DE
VENARUM O

1603

of

HIERONYMUS FABRICIUS
of AQUAPENDENTE
(1533?-1619)

FACSIMILE EDITION WITH INTRODUCTION, TRANSLATION, AND NOTES

*by*

K. J. FRANKLIN, D.M.

*Tutor and Lecturer in Physiology of Oriel College
and University Demonstrator of Pharmacology, Oxford*

RINGFIELD, ILLINOIS          BALTIMORE, MARYLAND

CHARLES C THOMAS

1933

HIERONYMVS FABRICIVS AB AQVAPENDENTE EQVES MEDICVS ET ANATOMICVS.

AUCULA ME GENUIT, TENET URBS PATAVINA. THEATRO SUM, TABULIS, FOETU, CLARUS ET OSTIOLIS.

TO

JOHN FARQUHAR FULTON

# CONTENTS

# LIST OF ILLUSTRATIONS

\*  \*  \*

NOTE.—For Reproductions of eight original plates in *De Venarum
Ostiolis*, 1505, see VII, pp. 77 ff.

# PREFACE

HAVE dedicated this book to Professor J. F. Fulton, as it was he who first suggested it, he who has throughout helped and encouraged me in its preparation. I hope that it will remind him, whenever he looks at it, of pleasant times in Oxford, and that it will assure him of the continued friendship of one who has greatly regretted his departure from Oxford.

*Il importe beaucoup de connoître l'Histoire de la Science à laquelle on s'attache.* There need therefore be no long *apologia* for a facsimile edition of *De venarum ostiolis*, for the discovery of the circulation by William Harvey was in large measure due to his correct estimate of the function of the venous valves, and about these he had heard while studying under Hieronymus Fabricius at Padua from 1600 to 1602 (1).* Robert Boyle wrote in 1688 (2) an account of a conversation with Harvey which is most pertinent here. "And I remember," he says, "that when I asked our famous *Harvey*, in the only Discourse I had with him, (which was but a while be fore he dyed) What were the things that induc'd him to think of a *Circulation of the Blood?* He answer'd me, that when he took notice that the Valves in the Veins of so many several Parts of the Body, were so Plac'd that they gave free passage to the Blood Towards the Heart, but oppos'd the passage of the Venal Blood the Contrary way: He was invited to imagine, that so Provident a Cause as Nature had not so Plac'd so many Valves without Design: and no Design seem'd more probable, than That, since the Blood could not well, because of the interposing Valves, be Sent by the Veins to the Limbs; it should be Sent through the Arteries, and Re-

* Figures in parentheses refer to entries in Chapter V, page 37.

[ 1 ]

turn through the Veins, whose Valves did not oppose its course that way."

Fabricius was not the first to mention the valves of veins, nor was he the first to publish a picture of a valve, but he *was* the first to demonstrate them publicly and to describe them in detail, and he therefore has the credit for making their presence an acknowledged fact of anatomy. "The true inventor is he who definitely places the world in full possession of knowledge and of facts of which one can every day and at will verify the reality and accuracy." Many have disparaged Fabricius for not realizing the physiological importance of his discovery, but in this, I think, they are unjust. It is an effort in research to break fresh ground, and, with the exhilaration that comes on finding something unknown before, there comes also very often a reaction, which seems to prevent one proceeding further oneself, and the next step is left to another. And it is the first step that is so hard to make. It is more charitable, also, to remember that Fabricius had many other activities, research in anatomy and surgery, the development of comparative anatomy, teaching, and a large medical and surgical practice, so that the venous valves were not all his care, and he may be pardoned for a too Galenical physiology. At all events, it was a happy coincidence for humanity that Fabricius was the most famous professor in the medical world at the time when Harvey was eager to further his medical studies, and that the young English student went therefore for two years to the University of Padua. For it is scarcely to be doubted that during this time Harvey was stimulated to an interest in those problems, by the elucidation of which he was afterwards to achieve immortality.

There are few more agreeable tasks than to acknowledge one's indebtedness to others, and in the preparation of this facsimile edition I have received generous help from many. Among these I may specially mention Professor Charles Singer, Sir D'Arcy Power, Dr. E. T. Withington, who kindly reviewed my translation and made a number of improvements in it, Dr. J. S. Prendergast,* who pointed out the passages which are Galenical in thought or origin, Mr. T. Gambier-Parry and Mr. Strickland Gibson of the Bodleian Library, Dr. Archibald Malloch, Librarian of the New York Academy of Medicine, and Major Hume of the Surgeon General's Library. But it is to the fellow-countrymen of Fabricius that this book owes most, and I wish here to thank Professor Castiglioni for allowing me to reproduce the architect's drawings of the anatomical theatre, Professor Capparoni for the information contained in his letters, Professor Dante Bertelli for permission to use his article on the anatomical theatre of Padua and the picture of it, and most of all Professor Favaro for a series of publications, which form my chief source of information about Fabricius.

To Mr. H. E. Powell, Librarian of the Royal Society of Medicine, I am indebted for the opportunity of photographing the copy of *De venarum ostiolis* which I used; the pages were removed from their binding and cleaned expressly for this purpose, and I was able to have them photographed before they were rebound, an invaluable privilege, especially as the large plate covers two pages.

To Dr. Arnold Chaplin, Harveian Librarian, and to Mr. W. J. Bishop, Assistant Librarian, of the Royal College of Physicians, are due my thanks for facilities for photographing the architect's drawings of the anatomical theatre. These drawings were prepared for the Harvey Tercentenary of 1928, and are now published, I believe, for the first time.

* The footnotes below the translation are Dr. Prendergast's.

[3]

Most of the photography which has been necessary has been done for me by Mr. Chesterman, of the University Department of Anatomy, Oxford, and I cannot estimate too highly the artistic way in which he has done it.

The frontispiece is reproduced from Tomasini, J. P., *Illustrium virorum elogia iconibus exornata*, Patavii, 1630, p. 133. The lines underneath are drawn from a separate source, *Aucula* being an old name for Aquapendente.

The translation I have left in its literal form when I might have made it more easy to read. This I have done for the following reasons  The original seemed to me to be written in somewhat crabbed Latin, although Fabricius had a good reputation as a classical scholar in his youth. I had a feeling that Fabricius' thoughts on the subject on which he was writing had not that clarity which comes with complete knowledge of the truth; it would be wrong, I think, to add a false appearance of such clarity in translating. He was quite incorrect about the function of the valves, and he relied too much on preconceived notions of the physiology of the blood's movement in his anatomical description, with the result that he altered some of his anatomical observations to fit these notions. Underlying all that he said, as Dr. Prendergast's footnotes reveal, was a traditional adherence to Galenical views, and it was this allegiance to authority that caused the confused thought which the style of the Latin reveals. Or so, at least, I think.

The word *ostiola* I have translated as "valves"; it is a difficult word to translate by any modern term which will give it its probable significance in the time of Fabricius. It refers, I imagine, to some well-known feature of the irrigation systems of the day, which had analogies with the current ideas of the movement of the blood.

Perhaps I may quote a passage written by Richard
Lower, which was published posthumously in John
Browne's *Myographia nova*, 1697, as it gives a synonym
for "valves," which is very probably a translation of the
word *ostiola*. If so, it is the only early translation of the
word which I have yet discovered. He says, "but the use
of all these *Vessels* will more clearly appear, if we consider the strange Artifice of certain *Valves*, or little
*Flood-gates* planted at these their Orifices." He is referring to the cardiac valves, it is true, but all the sug-
gestions I have seen as to the meaning of *ostiola* make
me think that he had this word in mind, and, in the absence of any more definite indication in the literature, I
put this forward as the best rendering into English.

The original text is in folio, and has been reduced to
the size of the present volume. Publication has been delayed for three years, owing to the crisis, but this only
renders the actual year more appropriate for the appearance of the book, as 1933 is in all probability the
quatercentenary of the birth of Fabricius. It is my hope
that Mr. Thomas may be justified in having undertaken
the financial risk, which in these days attends the publication of works on the history of medicine. I could not,
at all events, wish for a more considerate co-operator,
and I wish here to express my gratitude to him.

If I may, finally, give a reason for writing this book,
it is that I have a special interest in the circulation, and
more particularly in a rather neglected part of it, the
venous side. By translating *De venarum ostiolis* I have
made more accessible to the English and American
reader the work which was the precursor to Harvey's
book. Harvey's *De motu Cordis* is available in translation and in facsimile, and the next work of importance
in the story of the circulation, Richard Lower's *De Corde*
etc., London, 1669, is also now accessible in translation

and facsimile (14). These three works show the historical development of the subject, and lead on to the English writings of Stephen Hales and others, who were such able successors of these three great discoverers who went before them.

The rest of this book is arranged in the following order, namely, a biographical notice, the early history of work on the venous valves, a short account of the theatre of anatomy at Padua, a bibliographical note for which Professor J. F. Fulton is chiefly responsible, references, translation, facsimile, and reproductions of the original plates.

I am very grateful to the History of Science Society for its generous grant in aid of publication of this book.

# I
# BIOGRAPHICAL NOTICE

IERONYMUS FABRICIUS was born about 1533 at Aquapendente, near Orvieto, about half-way between Rome and Siena. His forbears had the rank of *Gonfalonierato* (standard-bearer) there, and were therefore considered noble in that locality; while his paternal grandfather, also named Hieronymus, once served as member of a legation from Aquapendente to the Pope. It is probable that Fabricius was the firstborn, as he took his grandfather's name, and at the time of his birth the family, though less prosperous than it had once been, was nevertheless not poor. His parents, as might be expected under these circumstances, brought him up with the care fitting to his station in life until about 1550, when he went to Padua, about two hundred miles away. Here he was received into the house of certain Venetian nobles, probably of the Lipaman family, and, with this great advantage, commenced his studies at the University, then probably the most famous in Italy. He began with Greek and Latin, and followed these up with Logic and Philosophy. The picture one has of him at this time is that of a young man gifted with great powers of memory, and a keen and penetrating mind. To those under whose protection he lived he was obedient, open, and sincere, and his pleasant manners and assiduity in the study of letters amply justified their patronage of him. His prowess in public and in private was beginning to mark him out when he turned his attention to medicine, and in this, as in many other circumstances of his life, he was befriended by fortune, for he studied under Gabriele Falloppio (1523–62), 'the Aesculapius of his age,' and an extremely able exponent of his subject. Falloppio's interest in his pupils' welfare is well known, and Fabricius soon won his friendship by the zeal he showed in his anatomical and surgical studies. About 1559 Fabricius presented himself to the Faculty for examination, and took his doctorate of Philosophy and Medicine. In 1562 his master Falloppio died, and from 1563 to 1565 we find Fabricius giving private lessons in anatomy. On 10 April in the latter year he was appointed by the Senate to the chair of surgery, on the understanding that he taught anatomy also, and the appointment was confirmed by ducal decree on 11 April. For this his salary was to be 100 florins a year.* The first course lasted from 18 December 1566 to 5 January 1567. In 1570 he entered among the promoters through the diploma of surgery, and on 29 October 1571 he received his first reappointment to the chair, his salary being increased to 200 florins a year. In 1574 he first saw valves in veins during the course of his dissection, and he has described the joy with which he found them. Ill most of the time in the winter of 1574–5, and again, this time with eye-trouble, in that of 1577–8, he only began to demonstrate the valves in 1578 (Bauhin) or 1579 (Alberti). In the interval he had, on 5 August 1577, made his first will so far discovered, and, on 4 October of the same year, had been reappointed a second time to his chair, with a further increase of salary to 400 florins a year. Somewhere about this time or earlier he had married Violante Vidal or Vidali, of Padua, for on 12 April 1578 she made her first will of which we know. His marriage was a very happy

* It is difficult to assign exact values to the currency, but the florin was probably equivalent to about eightpence in English exchange, and the *scudo* to about four shillings, while the ducat was of nearly the same value as the *scudo*, as far as I can ascertain. But I am quite open to accept a re-valuation of these figures. The fortune Fabricius left to his heiress was 200,000 ducats.

FIGURE I.

STATUE OF FABRICIUS IN AQUAPENDENTE
(For the photograph here reproduced the writer is indebted to
the kindness of Dr. Alfred E. Cohn, of the Hospital of the Rocke-
feller Institute for Medical Research.)

one, but there was, to Fabricius' increasing regret, no offspring from it. In 1584 he inaugurated anatomical teaching in a new theatre, which could be dismantled after use. On the fifth of February in the same year he received his third reappointment, at a salary of 600 florins, and the 12 May saw the successful conclusion of a dispute he had had with the College of Philosophy and Medicine, for on that date he was admitted into the College with all the privileges such admission entailed and gave up the lesser ones he had enjoyed since 1570 as a promoter through the licentiate in surgery.* The year 1585 saw the publication of his *Dissertatio de lue pestifera*. In January 1589 Fabricius had been annoyed by trouble during his anatomical course and had put it down to the German students. On 1 February he took the opportunity afforded by a lecture on the muscles of the tongue and the organs of speech to criticize the harsh and hesitant pronunciation of that nation, imitating almost *ad nauseam* their manner of speech in "Qui ƥonum ſinum piƥit, ſiu ſiſit" (Qui bonum vinum bibit diu vivit). It was not until October that he and they became reconciled. On 28 September 1589 he was reappointed to his chair a fourth time, at a salary of 850 florins. Pietro Paolo Biondi speaks of Fabricius in this year as being a married man, settled down in Padua in possession of riches sufficient for him to keep mules and coaches; he has lectured for many years, and still does so, in the University, is a superb anatomist, and is so famous that he is known simply, and without prefix, as Aquapendente. On 27 March 1590 he initiated surgical demon-

---

* An interesting parallel is found in the life of William Hunter, who in 1756 resigned, as was obligatory, his membership of the Corporation of Surgeons in order to become a Licentiate of the College of Physicians (Peachey, G. C., *A Memoir of William and John Hunter*, 1924, pp. 94 and 100).

strations, and in 1592 he published his work, *Penta-teuchos chirurgicum* etc., at Frankfurt. In the winter of 1592–3 he promised to interest himself in the reconstruction of the 'dismantlable' anatomical theatre, but in 1594 the permanent one was erected. On 28 September of this year he was again reappointed to his chair, this time at a salary of 1100 florins, and on 16 January 1595 he began his course in the permanent theatre. About 1596 was born his great-niece Semidea, whom he received later into his household and made his heiress, and who was the great comfort of his later years. Characteristically, Fabricius stipulated that her mother should stay away from Padua after he adopted Semidea; he says that her mother lived at a distance, and was much better at such a distance. Somewhere about 1596 or earlier Fabricius began to acquire an estate four miles outside Padua, at Bugazzi, and to build himself there a house and pleasure gardens, for it is recorded that Dario Varotari fell from a scaffold erected against the facade of *la Montagnola*, as it was named. In 1599 he acquired more ground for the estate.

In 1600 he published *De visione voce auditu* at Venice and Padua and *De formato foetu* at Padua. On the 24 September of this year a senatorial and ducal decree confirmed him in his chair for life, with the title of Supraordinary in Anatomy, and with a yearly stipend of 1000 scudi. In this year, too, William Harvey came to Padua. In 1601 he published, at Venice, *De locutione et eius instrumentis*. In the winter of 1602–3 he was often troubled with illness. In 1603 he published at Padua *De venarum ostiolis*, *De brutorum loquela*, *De gula de ventriculo* etc., and a second issue appeared in this year of *De locutione et eius instrumentis*. *De venarum ostiolis* he dedicated on 5 November 1603 to the German Nation of Arts, receiving in return from them two vessels of silver. The next year saw second publishings of *Penta-teuchos chirurgicum* and *De formato foetu*, and 1605 a second of *De visione voce auditu*, as well as *Consilia medica*, *De laesa mictione*, and *Chirurgy oder Wundartzney*. In 1606, November–December, he and Tommaso Minadoi attended Galileo in his illness, and in December he received thanks from the German students for his course in operative surgery. On the 5th of October 1607 five men, who were jealous of the reputation of Fra Paolo Sarpi, and strongly attached to the interests of the Pope, attempted the assassination of this brilliantly gifted man, and gave him three wounds. The Senate called Fabricius and Adrian Spigel to the bed of the wounded man, and in return for his services created Fabricius Knight of St. Mark. He returned to Venice on 1 January 1608 to receive the insignia of his knighthood. In the winter of 1607–8 he carried on lawsuits with Eustachio Rudio, Professor of Medicine at Padua, and was obliged to carry arms for his safety, but they became reconciled on 1 April 1608. In June he again attended Galileo. On the 25 August 1609, by senatorial and ducal decree, the chairs of surgery and of anatomy were separated, and Fabricius remained Supraordinary in Anatomy alone, retaining the salary of 1000 scudi, and delegating the surgical work to Julius Casserius. On the 14 November he again purchased additional ground for his country estate, and more in May of the next year. During the winter of 1612–3 he was almost continuously unwell, and in November 1613 finally retired from teaching, after fifty years of such work.* His retirement marked the be-

* There can be few who have occupied chairs for so many years. The late Professor Gerard Baldwin Brown, Honorary Fellow of Oriel College, who died 12 July 1932, was Watson-Gordon Professor of Fine Art in the University of Edinburgh from 1880 to 1930, a record only twice equalled in the history of that University (*The*

ginning of another spate of publishing. *De visione voce auditu* appeared for a third time in this year and a fourth in 1614, the first editions of *De gressu* etc. and *De musculi artificio* also saw the light in 1614; then came two publications of *De respiratione* in 1615, *Opera chirurgica* in 1617, *De motu locali animalium* etc., *De integumentis totius animalis*, and second editions of *De gula* and *De gressu* in 1618, and *De vulneribus Sclopetorum* in 1619. In 1614, on the 29 June, he organized a series of festivities at la Montagnola in honour of Andrea Morosini and other illustrious guests. This Sunday began with hunting, but the chief event was the sumptuous banquet and subsequent entertainment with which he indulged his guests. Rich gifts were made to them, and they returned at sunset to Padua, very satisfied, as letters show, with the hospitality they had received. In autumn Fabricius was in bed with a fever, but was better at Christmas. About 1615 he received a gold medal from Sigismund III, King of Poland. In November 1615 he was more or less seriously ill, and on the 9th of that month made his last will, which was, however, to receive many codicils before his death, three appearing in that year alone. On the 15 November 1617 appeared a biographical notice of Fabricius by Castellano, who added *"An adhuc superstes sit, ignoro."* At this time he was again seriously ill, but was quite well by April 1618 and attending to the printing of his books. On the 25 June, being once more seriously ill, he made his seventh codicil. His wife Violante probably died about 1618, and his great-niece Semidea was more than ever the comfort of the old man in his decline. She had, towards the end of 1615, attracted the attention of a Venetian youth of the Dolfin

*Times*, 14 July, 1932). Sir Edward Sharpey-Schafer has been Professor of Physiology for fifty years, though not all that time in the same chair.

family, perhaps had met him through his having studied medicine under her great-uncle. At all events it was the chief wish of Fabricius that their marriage should take place, but there was an obstacle, namely, the high rank of Daniele Dolfin. Fabricius was again ill in January 1619, and, fearing he had not much longer to live, he supplicated the Duke to decree that the descendants of his great-niece should be considered of noble rank, so that the two might wed. His efforts, conducted through intermediaries in March and April, met finally with success, and the marriage took place on 9 May in the chapel of Fabricius' own dwelling, so that the old man, despite his poor health, had the pleasure of being present, and achieved his ultimate purpose twelve days before his death. With the departure of his great-niece Fabricius had no longer any desire to live, and his last days were made more unhappy by the presence of relatives eager to become his heirs. He was taken ill on the 13th, and died at 6 p.m. on Tuesday, 21 May, 1619. He was buried on the 23rd in an unnamed grave in the western cloister of the Church of St. Francis, and his friend Johannes Thuilius Mariaemontanus delivered a magnificent funeral oration in the presence of the leading civic and academic dignitaries. *"Cecidit, heu cecidit, Hieronymus Fabricius ab Aquapendente, patriae suae decus, Medicinae lumen, Anatomiae restaurator, Chirurgiae parens, Gymnasii Patavini gloria, imo universae rei litterariae commune bonum. Una dies, una hora, unum temporis momentum abstulit, quod saecula non refarcient: praereptus est nobis ille Vir, quem qui aequent, nedum superent, communi omni iudicio vix reperiuntur. Lugeant igitur hunc casum communiter omnes, defleant hanc miseriam cives et peregrini, hunc interitum nemo non luctu et planctu prosequatur, et praestantissimum hunc virum hic iacentem conspiciens nullus non effundat uberrima lacrymarum flumina."*

Such, in brief, was the life of Fabricius, but there are many other aspects of it on which lack of space forbids one to enlarge, much as one would like to do so after reading the excellent accounts of Professor Favaro. A few points, however, may be briefly mentioned without encroaching too much on available space, and, in view of the ill-documented biographies that have appeared before the middle of the last century, perhaps they should be. Fabricius, though a superb anatomist, whose fame attracted to Padua students from all countries, was not an ideal lecturer on the subject. It is true that, when he was interested, he could give a marvellous lecture-demonstration, and many times he received the thanks of his students. But more often the reverse took place, and he seems often to have seized any excuse to cut short his course or to cancel it altogether. In pure anatomy, on the other hand, he was a master, and one must conclude that Fabricius was far better equipped for research than for teaching, and that his fame was due to the former rather than to the latter. It is clear that he was glad to give up teaching after fifty years in 1613, and the festivities at la Montagnola and the printing of his books, which followed soon after, seem to be signs of his joy at his liberation.

Nor was Fabricius quite the gentle person of the earlier biographers. He engaged in many lawsuits in the course of his life, and he had many quarrels with his students, especially the Germans. But his quarrels usually ended in reconciliation, and more than once he went out of his way to assist a German student. He seems to have belonged to that class of human beings who are not content with their own activity, but like to stimulate those around them, preferring even the anger of others to their placidity.

He intended to write a great work entitled, *Totius*

*animalis fabricae theatrum*, but this was not finished. Many of his works are chapters of this uncompleted work. He was the creator of comparative anatomy, for in his treatises he examines simultaneously the corresponding organs in man and in lower animals, to see what is common to all species and what differences exist among them. He left his illustrations of comparative anatomy to the State of Venice to be placed in the library. Osteology and myology, the study of the special senses, and embryology, were all advanced by his work. In surgery he improved both the instruments used and the operative technique. He gave the golden precept that the best surgeon is the one who cuts least, and with the greatest caution.* In the practice of medicine he did far more than earlier writers were willing to allow, as Professor Favaro has shown, and, if from the scientific point of view he was more eminent as a surgeon, yet his purely medical work brought him as much riches and renown as did his surgical, and perhaps even more.

It is interesting to see that both Fabricius, Harvey's scientific predecessor, and Richard Lower, Harvey's scientific successor, had panaceas. In the case of Fabricius, it was an aloes pill, about which Favaro gives detailed information (12). In that of Lower, it was barley-water (14).

This section would be incomplete without some reference to a recent, most interesting paper by Joseph Fritz (15) on "Polish Physicians who studied under H. Fabricius ab Aquapendente." The number of medical stu-

---

* cf. John Hunter. "Operations should never be introduced but in cases of absolute necessity. A Surgeon should never approach a victim for an operation but with humiliation: it is a reflection upon the healing art. He is then like the savage in arms, who performs by violence what a civilized nation would accomplish by stratagem." Peachey, G. C., *A Memoir of William and John Hunter*, 1924, p. 169.

dents inscribed in Padua in the sixteenth century was about ten thousand, and about ten per cent were Poles, so that they were second among foreign students to the Germans alone. Probably about three hundred Poles attended Fabricius' lectures, and practised anatomy under his direction, and there is little doubt, from the subsequent history of some of these, that the influence of Fabricius was of outstanding importance in the development of Polish medicine. The Polish students were a separate nation in Padua from 1592.

There is a manuscript in the University Library in Cracow, which was written by four Polish students in 1580/1, and which is a précis of Fabricius' lectures on surgery. Its correspondence in general features only with *Pentateuchos Chirurgicum*, 1592, shows "how the views of Fabricius on certain questions in surgery and anatomy developed and changed with time."

John Zamoyski, a former student and rector of the University of Padua, founded a new town, Zamosc, in Poland and wished candidates for medical teaching in his Academy to be educated at Padua. He was responsible for the presence in Padua of John Ursinus of Leopol, the most beloved pupil of Fabricius, who edited one of his first treatises, *De locutione et eius instrumentis liber*, 1601.

*De venarum ostiolis* is also connected with Ursinus. "Fabricius handed it to a certain Polish lady Edwiga Mielecka, who being in Italy is said to have evoked the admiration of medical professors in Padua by her great knowledge and who was also celebrated in Latin and Italian poetry. In the preface [to the Frankfurt edition of 1648] it is emphasized that she used to have long discussions with Fabricius and helped him in his investigations of problems of comparative anatomy by procuring scientific material from distant lands."

Ursinus lectured later on medicine at Zamosc, and in his *De ossibus humanis tractatus tres*, 1610, refers to Fabricius as "Praeceptor meus, omnium anatomicorum huius saeculi Parens." He died in 1613, and Zamoyski sent other pupils to Fabricius. The relations between these two distinguished men "became so close and friendly that Fabricius wished to dedicate his most famous work, the four books on anatomy, to Zamoyski, but this did not come to pass as Zamoyski died before they were finished. Instead of this he put his former intention into execution by dedicating it to the King of Poland Sigismund III, who was his patient. He also sent his medical prescriptions to the king by the intermediation of his pupil, the royal physician John Gallus of Bochnia, and having received the king's portrait as a sign of gratitude he dedicated his work on Surgery to him in the year 1618." In the dedication he says that, if life allows, he hopes also to dedicate to the king a further work on surgical instruments, with coloured pictures of morbid conditions in which their use is indicated. Unfortunately, death came to him before this projected work was accomplished.

Enough has been said, at any rate, to show what an enormous influence Fabricius had in the development of medicine throughout Europe, and the affection in which he was held in Poland and in Germany would have made him an outstanding figure in the history of medicine, even if he had not a greater claim to fame through having been the instructor of William Harvey.

# II
# THE EARLY HISTORY OF WORK
# ON THE VENOUS VALVES*

EFORE the sixteenth century no real knowledge of venous valves existed. Some have credited Hippocrates with a knowledge of such structures (16), but it is clear that he had no true appreciation of them (17). Others have thought that Rufus Ephesius knew of them, and so interpreted the word ἐπανθισμός of Dionysius Oxymachi (18), but this claim seems even less tenable. A stronger candidate for priority has been Erasistratus, but Dr. J. S. Prendergast, who has investigated very thoroughly Galen's ideas of the vascular system, explains away the views of previous authors (19). "The index-writer to Galen's works, vol. xxii, p. 299, says of Erasistratus, *venarum valvulas iam novit*. But where Galen speaks of membranes at the openings of the vessels he is referring, apparently, to the openings of the heart, e.g., in vol. ii, p. 203, and not to those of the veins. Cf. also vol. v, pp. 548–550." So one must conclude that Erasistratus was not the first to mention the venous valves. Petsche (20) attributed to Theodoretus, Bishop of Syria in the fifth century A.D., a knowledge of these structures, but the words of this divine, *Venas tenuissimis tunicis vestivit (Deus) et orificiis earum exilia opercula addidit*, scarcely convince a scientific mind.

It remains therefore to examine the work of the sixteenth century, and in doing this one must acknowledge

* In so far as this account corresponds with my *Valves in Veins: an historical Survey* (Proc. Roy. Soc. Med., 1927) I am grateful to the Secretary, the Royal Society of Medicine, for permission to republish.

[ 19 ]

one's debt to Dr. E. C. Streeter, who has written so admirably on this very subject in his historical note on Canano (21). If one were to go into details, one would have to reproduce, more or less fully, Dr. Streeter's account. I prefer to summarise what he says, in the hope that I may thereby persuade others to read the original, and so enjoy a masterful and sympathetic re-creation of a period in the history of medicine. The claim made on behalf of Canano as the first discoverer of the valves is a strong one, and was supported in their times by such authorities as Morgagni (22) and Haller (23). Briefly stated, it is as follows. About 1536 Giambattista Canano and his kinsman, Antonio Maria Canano, began demonstrating at Ferrara to an audience which included Piccolomini and Franciscus Vesalius, the brother of the great anatomist. In 1541 Giambattista Canano, then twenty-six years of age, became Professor of Anatomy at Ferrara, where he was visited between August and November by Vesalius. Four years after this, at Regensburg, and by the sick-bed of Lord Francesco d'Este, the two great anatomists met again. It was at this meeting that Canano told Vesalius of his discovery of valves in the opening of the azygos and renal veins, and of the veins overlying the upper part of the sacrum (24). Canano did not publish his results, and this meagre account, printed several years afterwards, may well be an incomplete statement of what he had done. From Amatus Lusitanus, who was at Ferrara from 1542 to 1548, comes further corroboration of Canano's knowledge of the azygos valves. Amatus stated that these were demonstrated at Ferrara, in 1547, to a large audience, the bodies of men and animals being used for the purpose (25). But Amatus, unfortunately, in publishing his work in 1551, said that the valve at the orifice of the azygos opposed the flow of blood from that vein into the vena

## DE VENARUM OSTIOLIS

cava, and he involved Canano's name in this erroneous idea. The leading anatomists, Vesalius (26), Eustachius, Falloppius, and also Franciscus Valesius, combined to pour scorn on Amatus, and as a result progress in the study of the valves generally received a set-back for several years.

Another claimant is Charles Estienne, who described *apophyses membranarum* in the liver veins in 1545, and who had observed them, according to Streeter, as early as 1538. These valves, said Estienne, opposed the backflow in the same way as the heart-valves. His description, however, is very vague, and he confines his observations to the liver veins. It is Estienne whose work Fabricius criticizes in his Explanation of Plate II (q.v.).

A third claimant is Jacobus Sylvius (1478–1555). In his *Isagoge*, published posthumously and in the year of his death, mention is made of valves at the mouth of the azygos, and often of other large vessels, such as the jugulars, brachial and crural veins, and the trunk of the cava as it leaves the liver. But Sylvius (27), in 1541, seems to have had no knowledge of these structures, and never claimed to have discovered them.*

Statements have also been made on behalf of Fra Paolo Sarpi, but these are negatived by Flourens (28) in a careful review.† Valves in the mesenteric veins are mentioned in the posthumous work of Realdo Colombo in 1559 (29).

Certain knowledge about the venous valves was therefore available to Fabricius, if he had read the earlier writings of the century, and his own teacher, Falloppius, had taken part in the dispute over the azygos

---

* Dr. E. T. Withington would like more credit to be given to Sylvius.

† The question cannot yet, however, be regarded as finally and conclusively answered.

valves. It comes as somewhat of a surprise, therefore, that he regarded himself as the first discoverer of these structures, and refers only to one previous worker, Estienne, whom he does not actually name, and whose work he mentions only to discredit it. "A discussion of these valves must be preceded by an expression of wonder at the way in which they have hitherto escaped the notice of Anatomists," says Fabricius, "both of our own and of earlier generations; so much so that not only have they never been mentioned, but no one even set eye on them till 1574, when to my great delight I saw them in the course of my dissection." But this statement was only published in 1603, and much may have dimmed the memory of Fabricius during his busy twenty-nine years in between. He was also often ill during the winter of 1602–3, and, if he wrote the book then, this may help to explain. Salomon Alberti, however, who wrote on valves in 1585 (30), and acknowledged his indebtedness to Fabricius, does also mention Canano and Amatus, and Fabricius refers to Salomon Alberti's work in his dedication of De venarum ostiolis, so it was open to him to give more credit to earlier workers. Perhaps Fabricius ignored these early accounts because they were so meagre, incomplete, and to some extent contradictory. If only these workers had given actual drawings of their discoveries, instead of merely describing their findings in words, things would have been different. Salomon Alberti actually was the first to print drawings of a valve, in 1585, and one cannot help feeling that papers on valves should always be plentifully illustrated so as to convey exact impressions of the findings which are described. On the 29th of February, 1579, Canano died in his sixty-fourth year (21). In the earlier part of this year Fabricius began public demonstrations of the valves in the veins of the extremities, according to Alberti, but in

1578, according to C. Bauhin (31). Thus five years elapsed between Fabricius' discovery of valves and his demonstration of them. This delay seems very long, but it must be remembered that Fabricius was very busy with other duties and that dissection was only practised in his times, for obvious reasons, for a short period in the cool of the year. He was also ill most of the winter of 1574-5, and was troubled with his eyes in the winter of 1577-8, so that his available time was not great, and one may assume that he began to demonstrate the valves as soon as he was really certain of his facts. It is possible

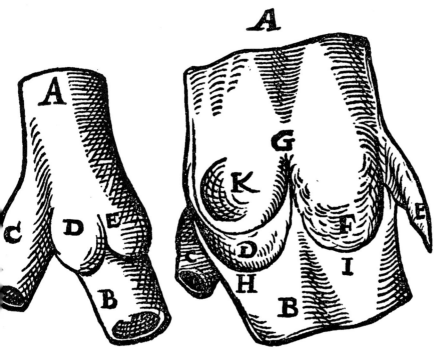

ꜰɪɢᴜʀᴇs 2 ᴀɴᴅ 3.—From Salomon Alberti, *De Valvulis* etc., 1585. Figure 1 shows the ꜰside of part of a leg-vein, *AB*, which receives a tributary vein, *C*, from a muscle. ꜰ are the valve sinuses. Figure 2 is of the same vein slit up longitudinally to show ꜰinternal arrangement. *ABC* are as in Figure 1. *D* is one cusp of the bicuspid valve. ꜰis the site from which the second cusp, *E*, has been partly cut away and reflected. ꜰis the cornu formed by the junction of the two cusps. *K* is the recess at the entry of ꜰtributary vein *C*. These two figures are the first drawings of a venous valve, and ꜰquite remarkably typical of such structures.

that Bauhin and Alberti both mean the same thing, that Fabricius demonstrated in the anatomical session of 1578–9. The course was of short duration as a rule and beginning at the end of one year went on for a short period into the next year. Actually the course began this winter on 16 January (17, pp. 112 and 120), owing to delay in the election of the *Massarii*. After demonstrating the valves, Fabricius waited twenty-four years before publishing his *De venarum ostiolis*, letting Salomon Alberti publish the first account of them and the first pictures of a valve (Figures 2 and 3) eighteen years before him. Truly conditions were different then! Fabricius, finally, in his published work, allowed analogy to supersede analysis in more than one instance, and adhered far too much in his interpretation to the ideas of Galen, even in one case translating the latter's actual wording. As a result of such inability to free himself from the traditions of the past, and to make correct deductions from accurate observations, he assigned to the valves many functions which have since been proved untrue, and Harvey holds that title to fame which might have belonged to his master, Fabricius.

Teatro anatomico di Girolamo Fabrici

FIGURE 4.—The anatomical theatre of Hieronymus Fabricius. The original occurs in Pietro Tosoni, *Della Anatomia degli antichi e della Scuola Anatomica Padovana*, Padova, 1844, and was photographed under the direction of Professor Dante Bertelli.

# III

# THE THEATRE OF THE
# SCHOOL OF ANATOMY
# OF PADUA

HE story begins with Alessandro Benedetti, who was born at Legnano in 1460, and died in Venice in 1525. His ability as a teacher of anatomy attracted large numbers of students, and, in order that they might profit to the full from his demonstrations, he made a large wooden structure on the lines of the Roman amphitheatre; this used to be dismantled after each course of lectures. An extraordinary number of students and distinguished persons came to these lectures, and they were even attended by the Emperor Maximilian himself. Tosoni, who wrote about the School of Anatomy of Padua in 1844, speaks of this theatre as "the oldest of all those whose memory is still with us."

Vesalius, Casserius, and Fabricius made use of theatres similar in construction to that of Benedetti, and, like his, capable of being dismantled when not in use. The reason they were made thus was that their position, until the time of Fabricius, was a variable one, on the ground outside the University building proper. Fabricius took his theatre inside to one of the upper rooms of the building; later on there was constructed in one such room the permanent anatomical theatre, which still bears his name. It is the oldest of such permanent structures.

A good photograph of this theatre, which will satisfactorily show all one would wish, cannot, owing to technical difficulties, be taken. To give some idea of it,

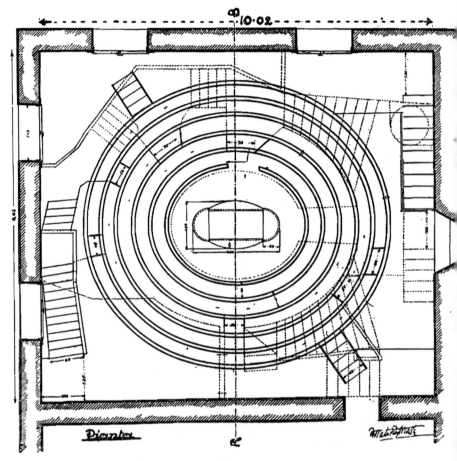

FIGURE 5.

FIGURES 5 AND 6.—Architect's drawings made at the suggestion of Charles Singer, and
the direction of Professor Castiglioni. The originals were exhibited at the Harvey T
tenary celebrations in 1928, and are now in the keeping of the Royal College of Phys
Figure 5 gives the plan, Figure 6 the elevation (along the dotted line *AB* of Figure 5),
anatomical lecture-theatre of Hieronymus Fabricius of Aquapendente. In Figure 5 1
emphasized one actual dimension (10.02 metres between the two arrows) at the top. In 1
6 I have also emphasized one actual dimension (5.40 metres between the two arrows)
top on the right.

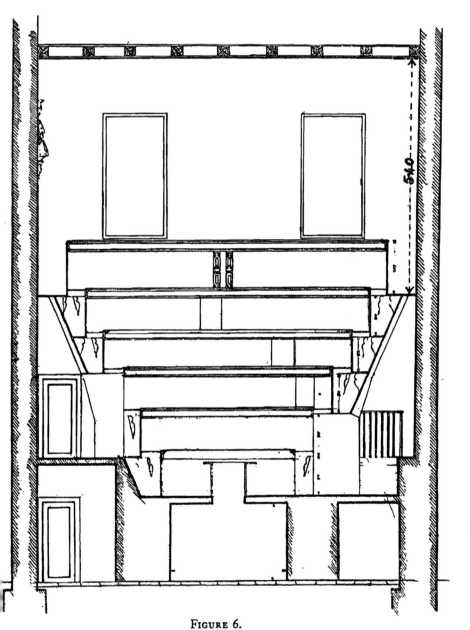

FIGURE 6.

I reproduce here a photo of an old drawing (Figure 4), and two architect's plans (Figures 5 and 6) made under Professor Castiglioni's direction at the suggestion of Professor Singer. The drawing gives a very exaggerated idea of the size of the theatre, and the plans are not equivalent to a picture. What one really wants is a drawing of the theatre from halfway up with the different galleries full of the right figures in sixteenth-century costume. Until the proper artist gives us this, these three plates and the accompanying information must be integrated in the mind of the individual reader. There were six concentric galleries so narrow that spectators had perforce to stand, so little above one another that the heads in one were only three feet above those in the one below. A tall man could not have stood upright without obscuring the view of the man behind and above him, and the head of the most distant spectator was only twenty-five feet away from the object of demonstration. The theatre held about three hundred people, and a calculation shows that there was just space for this number. In the small oval at the bottom was a table for the body or the part of it, which was to be dissected, and the space round this was reserved for the Professors of Anatomy, the Rectors of the City, the Rectors of the School, the Councillors and members of the medical College, and representatives of the Venetian nobility. Reference to the plans will show that these dignitaries could not have been present in any large number at a given time. The first gallery was occupied by the Councillors of the "Nations" (many mediaeval Universities were divided up into "Nations"),* and the ones above by students. The theatre was lighted by two

* Such division still survives in the University of Aberdeen. Jo. Aloys. Andrich published at Padua in 1892 *De Natione Anglica et Scota Juristarum Universitatis Patavinae 1221-1738.*

candelabra, each having three candles, and by eight lamps held by that number of students. Apart from this illumination the theatre was in darkness. Like many mediaeval structures it combined picturesqueness with what would be considered in modern times great discomfort. Yet in this room once resounded the voices of some of the greatest masters, such as Fabricius and Morgagni.

In 1844, two and a half centuries after its first building, it was lighted by means of several windows and in 1872 the teaching of anatomy was transferred to a new site. But the theatre of Fabricius remains as a perpetual monument to his name, and as a treasury of memories of the heroic days of Anatomy.

# HIERONYM.
## FABRICII
A B
## AQVAPENDENTE,
Equite Sancti Marci,

E T

# ANATOMICO SVPRAORDINARI
In Florentissimo Gimnasio Patauino.

# OPERA ANATOMICA·

De
- Formato Fœtu.
- Formatione Oui, & Pulli·
- Locutione, & eius Instrumentis.
- Brutorum Loquela.
- Venarum Ostiolis.

*CVM JNDICIBVS CAPITVM ET RERVM NOTAT*
*dignarum nouis, & copiosissimis.*

ET FIGVRIS ÆNEIS.

# PATAVII· MDCXXV

Sumptibus Antonij Meghetti.

FIGURE 7.—REPRODUCTION OF ONE GENERAL TITLE PAGE OF 1625.

IV

# BIBLIOGRAPHICAL NOTE CON- CERNING THE FIRST EDITION OF *DE VENARUM OSTIOLIS*

HE first edition of *De venarum ostiolis* offered a bibliographical problem of some interest, which has been solved by Professor J. F. Fulton and Mr. Strickland Gibson of the Bodleian Library. Nearly all copies of this tract are bound with other works of Fabricius under a general title-page bearing the date 1625, but the tract itself, if its title-page is present, bears the imprint "Ex Typographia Laurentij Pasquati, M.DC.III." It has been impossible to trace a copy of the work bound separately; but luckily there is presumptive evidence to indicate what constitutes a first edition. This evidence may now be presented.

In the Bodleian Library are four tracts of Fabricius bound together in an Oxford binding (Z. 4.6. Jur.). These tracts are, in order, *De formato foetu*, 1604, *De venarum ostiolis*, 1603, *De locutione*, 1603, and *De brutorum loquela*, 1603. There is no general title-page and, according to F. Madan's note, the title-page in front of *De formato foetu* is a faked one, which originally belonged to Fabricius' *De visione, voce, auditu* (Venetiis apud F. Bolzettam, 1600). The true title of the book has been cut out of the plate and "De formato foetu" on a new plate inserted in the old plate. The date "1600" has been altered by hand to "1620." Between this title-page and *De formato foetu* is interposed a dedication to Renatus Borromæus dated "Patavii, 2. Calend. Novemb. M.DC. VI." Each of the remaining tracts has a separate title-page. All four tracts have the same size of type-page, and the watermark is the same throughout, namely, a "trident-head" placed above a five-spoked "wheel," which has a "hub" of two circles and a "rim" of two somewhat distorted circles.* The faked title-page of *De formato foetu* has the same watermark, but that in the dedication to Renatus Borromæus is a five-pointed star, one point of which has been replaced by a series of knobs of diminishing size surmounted by a spike. This latter watermark is the same as one of the number found in *De formatione ovi et pulli*, 1621.

In the Bodleian Shelflist of 1616 onwards, the section Med. P. 2 has the following series of entries, in various hands:—

|     |                   |        |
| --- | ----------------- | ------ |
| 9.  | Pharmacopœia Lond. | [1618] |
| 10. | Pharmacopœia Aug. | [1613] |
| 11. | Hen. Petræus | [1615] |
| 12. | Fabr. ab Aqua | [1620] |
| 13. | Voellus | [1608] |
| 14. | Peccettius | [1616] |
| 15. | Fludd | [1619] |

Nos. 11 and 13 are no longer in Bodley, and Nos. 10–14 cannot be traced in the Binders' Book, but No. 9 was bound on 23 September 1618 and No. 15 on 19 November 1621, so it is a legitimate assumption that the four tracts of Fabricius ab Aquapendente were bound together between those dates, and that this copy of *De venarum ostiolis* is a first edition.

It may be suggested, therefore, that the marks of a first edition are a title-page, if present, as pictured on p. 48 of Fulton's *Readings in the History of Physiology*, a type-page of a particular size, and the watermark de-

---

* These details are not clearly seen in all cases, but they stand out in the specially cleaned copy of *De venarum ostiolis*, which belongs to the Royal Society of Medicine.

scribed above. The copy bound with Adrian Spigel's *De humani corporis fabrica*, Venetiis, 1627, in the Surgeon-General's Library has this title-page, and *possibly* this watermark, although only a "trident head," apparently, is visible, and the rough tracing of it kindly made for me by Major Hume shows some departure from the form which I have seen in all other copies.

Fabricius intended *De venarum ostiolis* and other tracts to be similar in format to the large work on animal structure which he never, unfortunately, completed. This striking and original plan is announced in the dedication of the tract:—"I have also made it," he says, "so that you, who await most eagerly of all these anatomical works of mine, may also be the first to learn that this pamphlet is that which shows the printer both the size of the page and the type of print of all the remaining pamphlets, and of that large work, which we are compiling on the structure of the animal as a whole. From this form no departure is allowed. The remaining pamphlets will be printed to this pattern, and thus young students, who have procured these pamphlets one by one on publication, and have arranged them in orderly sequence, will be able finally to put them all into one volume and bind them properly together without any unnecessary loss of text or money."

The sumptuously-printed folios which he published in 1603–4 were, therefore, issued separately and unbound. Though they escaped Choulant's notice, they are among the rarest and most beautiful works in the history of anatomical illustration. The plates are magnificent; in fact nothing on their scale had been seen since the days of Vesalius. However, after the first four had been struck off, some reason—perhaps the expense of printing or their failure to sell or his own ill-health—caused Fabricius to abandon the elaborate format of these earlier

[ 33 ]

publications, and later ones published in his lifetime, *De musculi artificio*, 1614, *De respiratione*, 1615, and *De motu locali animalium*, 1618, were all less extravagantly produced.

It is probable, then, that at Fabricius' death in 1619 there were a number of unsold copies of *De venarum ostiolis* and of the other three tracts left at the printer's. In 1621 *De formatione ovi et pulli* was published at Padua by another firm, with a type-page of the same size as that of these earlier tracts, but with different watermarks.

In 1625 A. Meglietti and R. Meglietti published separately at Padua bound collections of *De formato foetu*, *De locutione*, *De brutorum loquela*, *De formatione ovi et pulli*, and, with exceptions, *De venarum ostiolis*. A. Meglietti called his collection *Opera anatomica*, R. Meglietti called his *Opera physica anatomica*. They united thus, in the way Fabricius had intended, a number of his tracts. That the component parts were original editions is borne out by their similarity to those in the Bodleian book Z. 4.6. Jur. There are minor differences in the order of assembling the tracts, in the presence or absence of a separate title-page for *De venarum ostiolis*, in the inclusion or not of *De venarum ostiolis* in the table of contents on the general title-page, and finally in the presence or absence of the tract itself.

As regards *De venarum ostiolis*, the following variations occur in the copies of *Opera anatomica* detailed below. (1) It is mentioned on the general title-page as fifth in the list of tracts, and occurs in the book as the fourth, with a separate title-page as pictured on p. 48 of Fulton's *Readings in the History of Physiology*. Examples:—In the Royal College of Physicians and the Radcliffe Library. (2) It is similar to the above, except that it has no separate title-page. Example:—In the

Royal Society of Medicine. (3) It is not mentioned on the general title-page but is still present with a separate title-page. Examples:—In the Royal College of Surgeons of England and the New York Academy of Medicine. (4) It is not mentioned on the general title-page and is absent from the book. Examples:—In the Surgeon-General's Library and the British Museum. Copies of *Opera physica anatomica* are too rare for any similar analysis to be made of them

From all the above evidence one ventures to offer the suggestion that the sale of the first edition of *De venarum ostiolis* was comparatively small and that, as the tract was a large thin folio of only 23 pages, all unbound copies distributed were destroyed through use or else were bound with some work or works, not necessarily by Fabricius, but with the same or similar size of type-page. Those which were left unsold at the printer's were later acquired by the Meglietti and were assembled with Fabricius' other works until the supply of the original edition ran out; fewer general title-pages with *De venarum ostiolis* in the list of contents were printed than there were copies of the tract available, so some of the bound books contain the tract without its being mentioned on the general title-page.

Apart from the 1603 edition and the copies of it which were thus issued in *Opera anatomica*, 1625, or in *Opera physica anatomica*, 1625, *De venarum ostiolis* was also included in *Tractatus quatuor* fol., Francof., 1624, *Tractatus quatuor*, fol., Francof., 1648, *Opera omnia anatomica et physiologica*, fol., Lipsiae, 1687, and *Opera omnia anatomica et physiologica*, Lugd. Bat., 1738, the last year in which any of Fabricius' works were reprinted.

I have compiled as complete a bibliography as possible of the works of Fabricius, but fear to overburden this small volume by its inclusion. The long tale of

Latin, French, German, Italian and Spanish editions carried on the influence of the great master to a date more than two centuries later than his birth. It is certainly remarkable that John Hunter was ten years old when Fabricius' writings were last set up in type. The present translation of *De venarum ostiolis* is, I believe, the first English version to be published of any work of Fabricius.

# V
# REFERENCES

## I. PREFACE

1. ANDRICH. *De natione Anglica*, Padua, 1892, p. 46.
2. BOYLE, R. *A Disquisition about the Final Causes of Natural Things*, Lond., 1688, pp. 157–158.

## II. BIOGRAPHICAL NOTICE

3. THUILIUS, JOANNES (MARIAEMONTANUS). *Funus Perillustris, et Excellentissimi Viri, D. Hieronymi Fabricii ab Aquapendente etc. Die 23. Maij, Anno Epoches Christianae MDCXIX. in augusto templo Sancti Francisci, acerbo omnium luctu, celebratum.*
4. TOMASINI, JACOBUS PHILIPPUS. *Illustrium virorum elogia iconibus exornata*, Patavii, MDCXXX, pp. 313–320.
5. MAZZUCCHELLI, GIAMMARIA. *Gli Scrittori d'Italia*, vol. I, 1753, pp. 112ff.
6. PORTAL, A. *Histoire de l'Anatomie et de la Chirurgie*, tome II, Par., 1770, pp. 195–197.
7. FAVARO, G. *Il Terzo Centenario della Morte di Girolamo Fabrici d'Acquapendente*, Padova, Tipografia Giov. Batt. Randi, 1919.
8. *Idem.* "Sulle presenti condizioni delle Tavole di G. Fabrici d'Acquapendente," in *Monitore Zoologico Italiano*, Anno. XXXI, n. 8.
9. *Idem.* "Il restauro delle Tavole Fabriciane," in *Monitore Zoologico Italiano*, Anno XXXII.
10. *Idem. L'insegnamento anatomico di Girolamo Fabrici d'Acquapendente*, Venezia, premiate officine grafiche Carlo Ferrari, 1921.
11. *Idem.* "Contributi alla biografia di Girolamo Fabrici d'Acquapendente," Soc. Coop. Tip. Ed. Studentesca *La Garangola*, Padova, 1922.
12. *Idem.* "Girolamo Fabrici d'Acquapendente e la Medicina Pratica," *Bollettino Storico Italiano*

[ 37 ]

*dell'Arte Sanitaria* Appendice *Rassegna di Clinica,
Terapia e Scienze Affini* Anno xxvi, n. 1.—
Jan.–Feb. 1927.

13. CAPPARONI, P. *Profili Bio-bibliografici di Medici
e Naturalisti celebri Italiani dal sec. XV° al sec.
XVIII°*, 1926, pp. 35–37.

14. FRANKLIN, K. J. Gunther's *Early Science in Oxford*, vol. ix, 1932.

15. FRITZ, J. "Polish Physicians who studied under H.
Fabricius ab Aquapendente," *Janus*, May 1931.

### III. THE EARLY HISTORY OF WORK ON
### THE VENOUS VALVES

16. PORTAL, A. *Tableau chronologique d'Anatomie et de
Chirurgie,* in 10 above, tome vi, partie 1, p. 221.

17. HIPPOCRATES. *Opera omnia,* xxii, *De corde* §§ vii
and viii, xxiv, *De venis* §§ xviii-and xxiv.

18. RUFUS EPHESIUS. *De Corporis humani Partium
Appellationibus,* Lond. 1726 (ed. Clinch W.) p.
42.

19. PRENDERGAST, J. S. *Personal communication.*

20. PETSCHE, J. Z., in Haller's *Disput. Anat. Select.,*
vol. vi, pp. 762–786.

21. CUSHING, H., and STREETER, E. C. *Monumenta
Medica IV (Canano),* 1925.

22. MORGAGNI. *Epistola anatomica,* xv, in *Opera omnia,*
1765, ii, pp. 284–312.

23. HALLER, A. *Elementa Physiologiae Corporis Humani,* 1757, i, pp. 136–150.

24. VESALIUS, A. *Examen observationum Falloppii,*
1564, in Boerhaave ed. 1725, pp. 794–795.

25. AMATUS LUSITANUS. *Curationum medicinalium, cen-
turia prima, scholia curationis, 52,* 1551.

26. VESALIUS, A. *Fabrica,* 1555, lib. iii, c. iv, in fin.

27. VASSAEUS, J. *Anatomiae corporis humani tabulae
quatuor,* Lutetiae, 1540.

28. FLOURENS, P. *Histoire de la découverte de la circulation du sang,* 2nd éd., Paris, 1857, pp. 125ff.

29. COLOMBO, REALDO. *De re anatomica,* Venetiis, 1559,
lib. vi, p. 165.

30. ALBERTI, S. *De valvulis membraneis quorundam vasorum*, etc. In his: *Tres orationes*, etc., Norimb., 1585.
31. BAUHIN, C. *De corporis humani fabrica* Libri IIII. Basileae, 1592, lib. 2, cap. 50. Also 10 and 11 above.

## IV. THE THEATRE OF THE SCHOOL OF ANATOMY AT PADUA

32. BERTELLI, D. *I Teatri della Scuola Anatomica di Padova*, in *Numero Unico* published for the septencentenary of the University of Padua.
33. SINGER, C. Personal communications to the writer. Note 1. The plans are in the possession of the Royal College of Physicians.
    Note 2. For details of the anatomical teaching in the time of Fabricius, reference should be made to 10 above.

## V. BIBLIOGRAPHICAL NOTE

34. CHOULANT, J. F. *History of Bibliography of Anatomic Illustration*. Trans. by M. FRANK. Univ. Chicago Press, 1920. (German edition 1852.)

# VI

# THE TRANSLATION

# VALVES OF VEINS

by

## HIERONYMUS FABRICIUS
## of AQUAPENDENTE,
### ANATOMIST OF PADUA

PADUA:

*At the Press of Laurentius Pasquatus*

1 6 0 3

# TO THE ILLUSTRIOUS
# GERMAN NATION
from
## HIERONYMUS FABRICIUS, Greeting!

*hile I was pondering long since to whom, as well-wishing and indulgent towards me, I should most like to dedicate this pamphlet of mine on Valves of Veins, no one appeared more appropriate than the illustrious German Nation; as being the one which first of all looked on with me at this discovery of mine about the valves, shared my delight in their contemplation during dissection, and with me found in them a cause for wonder. You are they who have excelled all others in your zeal for Anatomy, and who value this branch of medicine so highly that it would seem the chief reason for your coming to Padua and frequenting this most celebrated school. So, on account of your most favourable disposition towards me, a disposition established by many most convincing proofs, I have rightly judged you the most fitting persons to whom I should offer this small gift as a mark of mutual good-will. Know, however, that I have also made it so that you, who await most eagerly of all these anatomical works of mine, may also be the first to learn that this pamphlet is that which shows the printer both the size of the page and the type of print of all the remaining pamphlets, and of that large work, which we are compiling on the structure of the animal as a whole. From this form no departure is allowed. The remaining pamphlets will be printed to this pattern, and thus young students,*

*who have procured these pamphlets one by one on publication, and have arranged them in orderly sequence, will be able finally to put them all into one volume and bind them properly together without any unnecessary loss of text or money.*

*If it surprises anyone that I am only issuing one part at a time and not producing the whole work at once, let him know that this plan ensures far greater accuracy in the individual pamphlets, since time is taken for revision, and the facts are carefully considered. This may cause delay, but it affects very markedly the finish of the whole work, which becomes in consequence both intrinsically finer and also more useful to the reader.*

*I have seen Salomon Alberti, your fellow-countryman, a man very learned on all sides, but especially keen and expert on Anatomy, write most learnedly on valves of veins; and with such honourable mention of me and praise of my name that, unless I wish to be discourteous, I must show him like affection and notice, and praise unceasingly the modesty of so great a man. And, because I approved of his work, I have deliberated more than once whether I could not conveniently omit this pamphlet, as he seemed to me to have written adequately on this very subject. But he is, on his own showing, fired by a singular desire, and exhorts and presses me to publish, and so I can no longer reasonably withhold it either from him, who shows me such affection, or from the many clever and learned young men of your nation, who never cease importuning me for it. Here, therefore, it now appears as a mark of gratitude to you, and as a help to all those whose pleasure is in such pursuits. Do you receive it cheerfully as a token of my grateful feeling towards you, and, seeing me so clearly yours, preserve for me always that same measure of goodwill which I now see you bearing me.*     *Farewell.*

# VALVES OF VEINS

by

## HIERONYMUS FABRICIUS
### of AQUAPENDENTE

Anatomist of Padua

ures
Pl.

fig.

ALVES of veins* is the name I give to some extremely delicate little membranes in the lumen of veins. They occur at intervals, singly or in pairs, especially in the limb veins. They open upwards in the direction of the main venous trunk, and are closed below, while, viewed from the outside †, they resemble the swellings in the stem and small branches of plants. *Valves a part of veins.*

*The shape of valves.*

My theory is that Nature[F1] has formed them to delay the blood to some extent, and to prevent the whole mass of it flooding into the feet, or hands and fingers, and collecting there. Two evils are thus avoided, namely, under-nutrition of the upper parts of the limbs, and a permanently swollen condition of the hands and feet. Valves were made, therefore, to ensure a really fair general distribution of the blood for the nutrition of the various parts. *The function of valves.*

A discussion of these valves must be preceded by an expression of wonder at the way in which they have hitherto escaped the notice of Anatomists, both of our own and of earlier generations; so much so that not only have they never been mentioned, but no one even set eye on them till 1574, when to my great delight I saw them in the course of my dissection. And this de- *The writer's first sight of valves.*

[F1] cf. Galen's frequent references to ἡ φύσις.

[ 47 ]

spite the fact that anatomy has claimed many distinguished men among its followers, men, moreover, whose
research was conducted with great care and attention
to detail. But a certain amount of justification does
exist for them in this case, for who would ever have
thought that membranous valves could be found in the
lumen of veins, especially as this lumen, designed for
the passage of blood to the whole body, should be free
for the free flow of the blood: just as in the case of the
arteries, which are valveless, yet, in so far as they are
channels for blood, are on the same footing as veins?

But a further justification can be advanced for the
anatomists. All veins are not provided with valves. The
vena cava *, when it traverses the trunk of the body, the internal jugulars †, and countless small ‡ super-
ficial veins in like manner, are destitute of them. On the
other hand, a reasonable charge may be made against
the earlier workers. Either they neglected to investigate
the function of the valves, a matter, one would think, of
primary importance, or else they failed to see them in
their actual demonstration of veins. For in the bare
veins exposed to view, but still uninjured, the valves in
a manner display themselves. Nay more, when assist-
ants pass a ligature round the limbs preparatory to
blood-letting, valves are quite obviously noticeable in
the arms and legs of the living subject §. And, indeed,
at intervals along the course of the veins certain knotty
swellings ¶ are visible from the outside; these are
caused by the valves. In some people, in fact, such as
porters and peasants, they appear to swell up like
varices: but here I must correct myself. It must be
clearly stated that actual varices are due entirely to the
dilatation of the valves and veins by too long retention
and thickening of the blood at the valves; since in the
absence of valves the veins would be expected to swell

*How the val-
ves of veins
shew up in
blood-letting.*

*The cause of
varices.*

up and dilate uniformly throughout their length,[F2] differing thus from varices. So that hereby another and that no mean function of the valves *may* come to light, namely, a strengthening action on the veins themselves. For as in cases of varix, with valvular incompetence or rupture as an expected finding, one always sees a greater or lesser degree of venous dilatation,[F3] one can doubtless say with safety that the Supreme Artificer[F4] made valves to prevent venous distension. Venous distension and dilatation would, moreover, have occurred readily since their coat is of membranous structure, single and delicate.[F5] And if they were to dilate, not only would the excessive accumulation of blood in them cause damage to themselves and the surrounding parts, and a swelling be caused, as is known to occur in cases of limb varix. There would also be a more or less defective nutrition of the parts above with the blood rushing in force, say, to a site of venous dilatation, and collected, as it were, in a pool. Arteries, on the other hand, had no need of valves, either to prevent distension—the thickness and strength of their coat suffices—or to delay the blood—an ebb and flow of blood goes on continuously within them.[F6] But let us, now, consider the number, shape, structure, site, distance, and other characteristics of valves. It was certainly necessary to make valves in the limb veins either of large or medium calibre—not the small ones—in order, no doubt, to slow the blood flow everywhere to an extent compatible with sufficient time being given for each small part to make use of the

*A second function of valves.*

*Why arteries have no valves.*

[F2] cf. Galen, vol. vii, p. 573.
[F3] cf. Galen, vol. vii, p. 730: vol. x, p. 943.
[F4] cf. Galen's frequent references to ὁ δημιουργός, e.g., vol. iii, pp. 237–8.
[F5] cf. Galen, vol. ii, p. 601: vol. iii, p. 457.
[F6] cf. Galen, vol. ii, pp. 196, 210.

nourishment provided. Otherwise the whole mass of blood, owing to the slope of the limbs, would flood into their extremities,[F7] and collect there, causing a swelling of these lower parts, and wasting of the parts above.

*Valves slow the blood.* That the blood flow is slowed by the valves, evident even without this from their actual construction, can be tested by anyone either in the exposed veins of the cadaver, or in the living subject if he passes a ligature round the limbs as in blood-letting. For if one tries to exert pressure on the blood, or to push it along by rubbing from above downwards, one will clearly see it held up and delayed by the valves. This indeed was the

*How the writer was first led to observe valves.* way in which I was led to an observation of such nature. Small veins, however, had no need of valves, for two reasons. First, owing to their smallness, they held only a little blood and all that suffices for them: and secondly, it was sufficient for the nutriment to delay in the larger vessels as in a fountain-head, since by this means the small tributaries also would not lack what was necessary.

*The need of valves in the limbs.* In the limbs, on the other hand, there was some need of valves. The legs and arms are very often engaged in local movement; this movement is at times vigorous and extremely powerful, and in consequence there is a very large and vigorous output of heat in them. There is no doubt that with this output of heat the blood would have flowed to the limbs and been drawn to them in such an amount that one of two things would have happened. The principal organs would have been robbed

*The reason why the chief organs should have a copious blood supply.* of their nutriment from the vena cava, or the limb vessels would have been in danger of rupture. Either alternative would have been fraught with very serious

[F7] Galen got over this difficulty by supposing that there was a vital "attractive" power in the various tissues, and that blood only went where it was wanted.

ill for the animal as a whole, since the principal organs, such as the liver, heart, lungs and brain, had constant need of a very plenteous blood-supply. It was for this

K.L. reason, I imagine, that the vena cava (*), in its passage
.I B. through the trunk, and likewise the jugulars (†), were
made completely valveless. For the brain, heart, lungs, liver and kidneys, which are concerned with the welfare of the body as a whole, needed to be well-supplied with nutriment, and absence of even the briefest delay was essential, if lost substance was to be restored, and vital and animal spirits, by the agency of which animals continue to live, were to be generated. If, however, by chance you see valves at the beginning of the jugular

*A possible function of valves in the jugulars.*

veins‡ in man, you may say they have been placed there to stop the blood rushing in spate to the brain, and collecting therein in undue amount, in the downward position of the head. For the reasons enumerated, then, valves were given to the medium and large sized veins though not to the small ones, in the limbs, and yet were not given to the trunk of the vena cava or to the jugulars. Though indeed valves have been put in

f the very many places, where, for instance,§ smaller branches
espe- leave the main stem to continue in other directions, and
.IV
). this is a mark of rare wisdom, the object being, I imagine, that the blood may be delayed at that point where it needs distributing to other parts; whereas, without such an arrangement, it would doubtless have flowed in mass through the single wider and straighter venous channel. Valves are present, so to speak, as intelligent doorkeepers of the many parts, to prevent escape of the nutriment downwards, until the parts above have acquired their fitting share of it.

*The site of valves.*

The shape of valves is such that they resemble the nail of the index or other three fingers. They open upwards in the direction of the main stem of the veins,

*The shape of valves.*

while below and at the sides they are united to the vein-wall. Further, if one has seen the valves in the heart,*   *Pl.
or those of the great artery or arterial vein, one will
have got a fairly accurate picture of the shape of all
*The distinction between cardiac and venous valves.* these venous valves, except that the cardiac ones are
three-fold,[F8] while the venous ones occur singly or in
pairs in their respective situations. In like manner the
cardiac valves were made very thick to meet the de-
mands of diastole and systole,[F9] while the venous ones
*The reason for the extreme delicacy of the valve-membrane.* are extremely delicate. The valve membrane is thus
delicate because it was unfitting for the blood's place
to be largely occupied by membranes, and this would
undoubtedly have occurred, had the valves been made
too thick in this respect. But also deserving of comment
is the fact that this extreme delicacy goes hand in hand
*The reason for the extreme toughness of valves.* with extreme toughness. This was done for the safety
of the valves, and to obviate any risk of damage; that
is to say, to prevent such valves being ruptured by a
sudden strong rush of blood against them. The toughness and strength of these same valves are well exempli-
fied by varices. For if they hold back and support for
a long time, a tough, thick, inspissated blood such as
the melancholic,[F10] one is forced to concede that these
membranes are strong. Indeed, anyone, attempting
even with some effort to push the blood down through
the veins, would feel the resistance and power of the
valves.

*The number of valves.*   Double valves† were put at intervals in individual   †M
places, not triple ones as in the heart, because in the   Pla
heart it was more a question of preventing reflux of
blood,[F11] in the veins, on the other hand, of delaying in

---

[F8] cf. Galen, vol. ii, p. 617: vol. iii, pp. 477 and 461.
[F9] cf. Galen, vol. iii, p. 486.
[F10] cf. Galen, vol. v, p. 118: vol. vi, p. 815.
[F11] cf. Galen, vol. iii, pp. 476–478.

some measure its passage. In the heart, again, a large diastole and systole were present, in the veins none. Finally, in the heart the openings are very great and channels very large in which valves are found; and for this reason triple valves have sometimes been seen in [the veins of] the ox, presumably on account of the great size of this animal.

If indeed double valves were adequate for veins, the provision of triple ones would have been pointless. But double ones were adequate because double ones were competent to slow somewhat the strong flow of blood, and yet in no wise to prevent its passage. For this reason, at intervals, not a few places are found with but a single valve in each,* the object being, undoubtedly, to grade with extreme accuracy the slowing of the blood. Where need of delay was greater, two valves were put, where less, one only. But the situation of choice for a single valve† is where nature is about to give off a somewhat smaller vessel obliquely from a larger branch. In such a case a valve is made like a floodgate in the larger branch, a little below the opening of the smaller one which is given off from it. Thus, doubtless, the descending blood is not only held back by the valve, but, striking on it, floods backwards, and, pooling, enters the mouth of the small vein.

The activity which Nature has here devised is strangely like that which artificial means have produced in the machinery of mills. Here engineers put certain hindrances in the water's way so that a large quantity of it may be kept back and accumulate for the use of the milling machinery. These hindrances are called in Latin *septa* (sluices) and *claustra* (dams), but in dialect *clausae* and *rostae*. Behind them collects in a suitable hollow a large head of water and finally all that is required. In like manner nature labours in the veins by

*The reason venous valves are usually paired.*

*The reason why they are single in certain veins.*

*Analogy between valves and the devices which hold back the water in mills.*

means of valves, here singly, there in pairs, the veins themselves representing the channels for the streams. [F12]

*The site of valves.* Nor let anyone here be surprised that nature puts valves—frequently paired—in various places,* where no branch is given off obliquely in the trunk of a vein, while nevertheless valves are required to hold back the blood somewhat and retain it. For valves are placed in veins less with a view to causing a pooling and storing of blood before the oblique mouths of branches than with a view to checking it on its course and preventing the whole mass of it slipping headlong down and escaping. A row of many valves was needed, and individual ones contributing each a little, not only to delaying the hurrying blood as already described, but also everywhere to preventing distension of the veins.

*P and wh*

Here again indeed one may fairly wonder at Nature's activity, for two valves† are made very close to one another, and so large that they take and fill up more than half of the vein-lumen: the remaining half is free and completely valveless. So nothing was in a position to prevent the blood from being able to flow in mass through the free part of the vessel, and causing the in-

†P 2.

*The interval between valves.* conveniences already described. Nature, therefore, besides providing very many valves at intervals of two, three, or four fingers along the length of a vessel, devised further an ingenious mechanism to slow the strong current of blood. More valves, placed along the same side or in a straight line, would have caused either no delay or else quite a negligible one, as the blood would have flowed straight through the free part of the vessel. On the other hand, had she filled the whole lumen in individual places with three or four valves, she would

[F12] cf. simile employed by Galen, vol. ii, p. 210, by Aristotle, *P.A.*, vol. iii, p. 668ᵇ, and by Plato, *Tim.*, xxxv, of irrigation system to illustrate blood-flow. cf. also Harvey's water-pump.

have completely stopped the passage of the blood.
Nature has therefore so placed the valves that in every *How the val-*
case the higher valves are on the opposite side of the *ves are placed.*
vein to the valves immediately below them; not unlike
fig. the way in which in the vegetable kingdom* flowers,
leaves, and branches grow successively from opposite
figs. sides of the stem. In this way the lower valves† always
delay whatever slips past the upper ones, but mean-
while the passage of blood is not blocked.

Finally, a point in connection with valves needs in- *The reason*
vestigation, namely, how it happens that in some people *letting more*
more frequent and more numerous valves are seen in *in some per-*
both legs and arms, in others fewer; a fact which is *sons, in others*
very noticeable when attendants pass ligatures round *fewer.*
the limbs in the living person for the purpose of blood-
letting. It must be said that more are seen in such as
have much, very thick melancholic blood, or alterna-
tively very thin, bilious blood (in which cases there is
over-functioning of the valves, either to delay the thin
fluid blood in the one case, or, in the other, to prevent
the thick blood from distending the vein). Or again
more are seen in such as are of powerful build or in-
clined to flesh, and to that extent have more numerous
veins, so that they need greater functioning of valves
to provide blood for the oblique branches. Or have very
wide vessels which demand many valves better to delay
the current of blood and increase the strength of the
veins. Or the parts receive long straight veins [and more
valves are present] so that the length and straightness
should not allow the blood to rush right along in a
stream, undelayed. Or finally more valves occur if an
animal is naturally rather agile in its movement. And
such is the wisdom and ingenuity of Nature which by
my own efforts I have discovered in this new field. The
number of valves in each vein, their distribution in the

[ 55 ]

*Plates of val-* tissues, and all other matters will become better known
*ves a neces-* from an actual inspection of the Plates than from any
*sity.*
written account.[F13]

[F13] This is not in the Galenic manner. Galen repeatedly refers to
the advantage of ocular inspection of *dissections*. cf. also Aristotle's
reference to anatomical schemes and illustrations, a method of
study much in use until Galen's day.

# EXPLANATION OF PLATE I ON
# VALVES OF VEINS

*P*LATE *I shows some valves of veins in about half of an arm. We have chosen to give complete details of all the valves in the leg only, to prevent this small pamphlet from becoming unwieldy with the number of its figures. First, therefore, at the origin of the internal jugular, that is, at the lower end of the neck, there are twin valves A., and in front of them a very large vein-mouth, E.E.; but in the jugular A.B.D., apart from this, no other things are visible, above these two valves A. already mentioned, except a gland below the ear D.; and in the branch B.C. no valve is present, only a medium-sized vein-mouth. In the axillary vein, F.G., however, after the twin-valves A., there follows one large valve H. Thereafter, the axillary vein F.G. having divided into the cephalic or humeral vein G.I., and the basilic or iecoraria G.K., there are present in the cephalic G.I., where it passes through the outer part of the arm under the deltoid muscle L.R.M.I., two valves L. & M. They are separated by about five fingers from one another, and the first L. is situated at the beginning of the deltoid L.R.M.I., the second M. at its end. In the basilic or hepatic vein G.K., on the other hand, as it proceeds through the inner part of the arm, four valves N.O.P.Q. of moderate size are placed. Of these the second O. is separated from the first N. by an interval of four fingers; the third P. from the second O. by one of three fingers; the fourth Q. from the third P. by one of two, and then follow two small valves K.*

*In this figure, in addition, the following are marked:—*
*S.S.S.S.S. Five divided ribs.*
*T. The axilla or wing of the arm.*
*V. The muscle commonly called 'The Fish.'*

# EXPLANATION OF PLATE II ON
# VALVES OF VEINS

*PLATE II, which is the largest of all, and especially necessary, contains five figures.*

*Figure I shews a living arm, bound above with a ligature, as usually happens in blood-letting. In it there is seen part of the cephalic or humeral vein A.B., and part of the basilic or iecoraria C.D., then the vena Communis popularly called Median E.F., in which, as in other veins, valves O.O.O. are seen like so many knots. For this is the kind of picture the valves present in living arms when viewed from the outside.*

*Figure II presents two veins of the legs, A.B. and C.D., turned inside out to show how the valves O.O.O. are placed in the lumen of the veins. From an inspection of these everted veins one particular thing is especially clear, namely, that the earlier and upper valves are situated on the opposite side to those next in succession to them; branches in plants behave similarly, as will be shewn in Figure III. In this Figure, secondly, it should be noticed that in the first or upper leg-vein A.B. the valves O.O.O. have been plugged with cotton-wool so that they should be better seen: but in the second leg-vein C.D. the valves O.O.O. are empty.*

*In Figure III knots N.N.N. formed by the cutting off of the branches of a plant are seen, and it is placed immediately below the last, as we pointed out in describing Figure II, to facilitate comparison between valves and the origin of branches.*

*Figure IV shows the plant called Verbena. It is this plant, popularly very well known, from which, in Figure III, the branches have been cut.*

*Figure V is of a liver A.A. dissected to show the trunks of the vena cava B.B.B.B. and vena portae C.C.C. near the gall bladder D., as well as the first comparatively large branches of each vein. This was done specially to let students observe that the statements handed down by one who wrote before me do not conform to the facts as shewn by dissection. That is to say, where he states that in the trunks and offshoots of the vena cava B.B.B.B. and vena portae C.C.C., as they emerge from the liver A.A., are to be found "apophyses membranarum," similar to the valves present in the heart. For from this description anyone might well have thought that valves are present in the trunks and offshoots of the aforesaid veins, whereas actually none are visible, but large branches, the apertures of which are seen, arise at once from the trunk of each vein, that is to say, of the Portal C.C.C. and Cava B.B.B.B., without any delay, and are distributed internally to the liver A.A. substance.*

# EXPLANATION OF PLATE III ON
# VALVES OF VEINS

*PLATE III shows in its upper part the heart A.B.C. This has been divided at the left ventricle A.D.E.C. to show its fibres D.E., and the three valves F.F.F. at the origin of the aorta or great artery G.H.I. To show further in the large artery G.H.I., which has been slit up along its whole length throughout the trunk of the body, the very numerous apertures which occur between its upper and lower portions. These are nothing else than branches of this same vessel distributed to the parts of the spine and elsewhere. This great artery obviously contains no valves, nor likewise do the other vessels, its branches. But the vena cava K.L.M.N. also, where it passes through the trunk of the body side by side with the great artery F.G.H.I. and is single and at its largest, is equally unprovided with any valves; for this reason it has here been slit up throughout its length. In its upper part, however, there are present two large apertures R. & S. which open into the liver. These are followed soon after by a lower aperture M. belonging to the right renal vein, and a little lower still the opened left renal vein O. is seen, leading to the left kidney P. and destitute of valves.*

# EXPLANATION OF PLATE IV ON VALVES OF VEINS

*P*LATE *IV, and the first of the leg, contains two figures, which show us, on the inner aspect of the whole leg from the hip almost to the foot, the valves of two branches. Of these one, AB.BG., is the inner and somewhat larger, the other, DE.EH., the outer and slightly smaller. The inner AB.BG. is seen to be nearer the ham of the knee I. It has five valves L.M.N.O.P. distributed at fixed intervals in such a way that single valves only are present from the upper part A. to the lower part P., where the vein has gone past much of the ham of the knee I. and of the knee itself K. Afterwards from Q. to B. follow twin valves in Figure I.; and in Figure II at the bottom of the leg, near the foot, is present only one valve R. And all the valves which occur in the obliquely-distributed branch LMNOP and in Figure II RG. are single except Q. and B., which are double.*

*The second, outer, branch D.E. proceeds from the front of the hip and is nearer to the knee K. It goes forward a little way from D. and its first provision of valves, twin ones, is at S: from S. to below the knee it has four valves T.V.X.Z. These are indeed all single, but yet so placed that three, T.V.X., are separated from each other by intervals of two fingers, while the fourth Z. is four fingers distant from the third X. And where the twin-valves S. occur at the beginning, and at the end the valve Z., there a branch is given off obliquely, but not at the other intervening valves T.V.X.*

# EXPLANATION OF PLATE V ON
# VALVES OF VEINS

*P*LATE *V is so connected with the two following plates,
namely, VI and VII, that if you had joined to the
lower end B.C. of Plate V the upper end B.C. of Plate
VI, and thereafter to the lower end D. of Plate VI the
upper end D. of Plate VII, you would have put together
the whole human leg A.B.C.D.E. And in this composite
picture you would see at one glance many valves of the
whole leg, partly on the inside and partly on the outside.
These you will now see separately in the individual plates.*

*Thus the figure depicted in Plate V shows both the vein
and the artery of the hip. They are slit open from their
bifurcations I.K.L.M. & A.H.F.G. throughout their
length, so that you may see that the vein I.K.L.M.N.B.N.C.
has valves, but that the artery A.H.F.G. is completely de-
void of them. The vein LM, then, where it is still single,
i.e. almost up to the groin M.O., receives a pair of valves;
after its division into two, N.B.N.C., the deeper and
larger part N.C. has twin-valves in two places at about four
fingers' distance, and then is hidden from view at C. The
smaller part, on the other hand, contains twin-valves at
the beginning N. of the bifurcation; then at two fingers'
interval another set of twin-valves; again after a space of
three fingers another set, and in the fourth place, finally,
stands a single valve at a distance of four fingers; this the
figure depicted in Plate VI will show.*

# EXPLANATION OF PLATE VI ON VALVES OF VEINS

*PLATE VI is continuous at B.C. with the preceding one, and shows a single vein only B.P.Q.R.S.T.D. This vein is part of the smaller branch and comes from the bifurcation of the vein described in Plate V to constitute the Saphena. In it occurs at once a single valve P., which is placed fourth, at a distance of four fingers, among the valves described in the preceding Plate. Then along from this valve P. are seen twin-valves Q., having in front of them. α.β. a small obliquely coursing branch. After this, at an interval of four fingers and almost under the ham of the knee, twin-valves R. are again seen, but without any branch. Below these, at an interval of three fingers, is disclosed a single valve S., but it has in front of it a small oblique branch γ.δ.ε. And four fingers again from this valve S. is present another valve T., which also has in front of it a small branch ζ. η. Finally, at a distance of about five fingers, and in the following figure, continuous with the present plate at D, you will see a valve present, if you turn over the page.*

# EXPLANATION OF PLATE VII ON VALVES OF VEINS

*PLATE VII, continuous with the preceding one at D., has, in the same Saphena D.E., at a distance of about five fingers from the last valve in the preceding Plate, a valve V. with its obliquely coursing branch θ.ι. in front of it. It then shows the valves XYZ of the whole foot as they are distributed through this member high up on the inner aspect. In the first place, it shows at the heel κ.λ. twin-valves X, which have on opposite sides the openings of two branch-veins κ.μ.λ.ε. At an interval of about three fingers from this twin-valve X, a single valve Y is present, with a tributary ξ running off in front of it; and at about the same distance again the last valve Z of the same Saphena is seen, again with a tributary rising close to it, but not in the same position as the tributary ξ. Finally, the vein Z.E. runs forward without any valves right up to the extreme tip of the large toe, forming the end of the Saphena.*

# EXPLANATION OF PLATE VIII ON VALVES OF VEINS

*P*LATE VIII shows the valves of the larger part of that branch which went forward from the bifurcation of the vein travelling with the artery and already described in Plate V, which was the second of the Plates on the leg. It is the larger internal branch A.B. of that vein which, running inwards towards the inner part of the hip in company with the large branch of the artery B.C., proceeds as pictured in this Plate, and exhibits all these valves D.E.F.G.H.I. First it shows twin-valves B., with a small branch α; then a further set of twin-valves E. with a small branch β: in the third place, at the knee K., a large single valve F. with a small branch γ. given off in front of it: in the fourth place, at the fleshy part L. of the leg which is called the calf, twin-valves G. without any small branch: in the fifth place a single valve H. with its accompanying small branches δ.ε.: in the sixth place twin-valves I. without small branches; and below these the vein divides into two, B.M. and B.N.

And because these plates here displayed are sufficient of themselves to demonstrate the wonderful activity Nature has employed in the production of valves, we have considered it right to forbear from picturing the other remaining ones, here making an end.

# VII
## THE FACSIMILE AND REPRODUCTIONS OF THE ORIGINAL PLATES

# HIERONYMI FABRICI

## A B

# AQVAPENDENTE

## ANATOMICI

## PATAVINI

## D E

# VENARVM

## OSTIOLIS.

## PATAVII,

Ex Typographia Laurentij Pasquati.

## M D C. I I I.

# INCLYTAE
## NATIONI
# GERMANICÆ.

### Hieronymus Fabricius. S. D.

 Ogitanti mihi iamdudum, cui potiſſimum, tanquam beneuolo & fautori, hunc
meum de Venarum Oſtiolis tractatum dicarem, nullus ſuccurrit, cui magis eum conuenire exiſtimarem, quàm Inclytæ Nationi Germanicæ; vt
quæ inter cæteras hoc meum de iiſdem Oſtiolis inuentum prima mecum ob-
ſeruarit, mecum in ſectione corporum iucundè contemplata ſit, mecum ad-
mirata. Vos ij eſtis, qui præter cæteros Anatomen expetiſtis; quique
hanc medicinæ partem tanti facitis, vt vel huius potiſſimum cauſa Pata-
uium acceſſiſſe, & Florentiſſimum hoc Gymnaſium frequentaſſe videamini;
vt iure egò vos digniſſimos eſſe cenſuerim, quibus pro veſtra propenſiſſima in me voluntate, multis,
ijsꝗ certiſſimis confirmata indicijs, munuſculum hoc, tanquam mutuæ beneuolentiæ ſignum, offer-
rem. Quod ipſum tamen ea quoꝗ ratione ſcitote à me eſſe factum, vt vos, qui ex omnibus primi
boſce meos de Anatome labores audiſſimè exſpectatis, primi quoꝗ intelligatis hunc tractatum eſſe
enim, qui cæterorum tractatuum, magniꝗ illius, quod de totius animalis fabrica molimur, operis,
impreſſori tum chartæ magnitudinem, tum charactorys formam, demonſtret, à qua diſcedere non li-
ceat. Etenim ad hoc veluti exemplar cæteri imprimentur tractatus, quo poſſint adoleſcentes, vbi
ſingulatim eos, vt quisꝗ editur, ſibi comparârint ſuáque locis collocarint ac diſpoſuerint, tandem
vniuerſos in vnum volumen coniectos apte compingere & colligare ſine vlla aut libri, aut impenſæ,
iactura. Cæterum ſiquis eſt, qui miretur ſingulas tantum partes à me prælo ſubijci, non totùm ſemel opus emitti, is ſciat, hac ratione ſumpto ad recognoſcendum ſpatio, & rebus diligenter penſita-
tis, ſingulos tractatus longè fieri exactiores, atꝗ hoc, quicquid eſt moræ, ad totius operis perfe-
ctionem, & maiorem tum ipſius dignitatem, tum Lectoris vtilitatem, vehementer pertinere.
Vidi ego Solomonem Albertum veſtrum Germanum, virum vt vndecunꝗ doctiſſimis, ita Ana-
tomes in primis & ſtudioſum & peritum, de Oſtiolis venarum doctiſſimè ſcripſiſſe; cum tam bono
rifica mei mentione, tantaꝗ nominis mei laude, vt, ni inhumanus eſſe velim, non & ipſe eum mu-
tuo diligere, & obſeruare, ac perpetuo etiam laudare tanti viri probitatem, non poſſim. Et quoniam
opus placuit, dubitaui non ſemel, poſſetne hic tractatus commode à me omitti; quod ſatis luculen-
ter ille de hac ipſa re ſcripſiſſe mihi videretur. Sed quoniam ipſe mirifica ſe eius incenſum eſſe cupi
ditate oſtendit, meꝗ vehementer, vt edam, hortatur atꝗ vrget, diutius iam debere nec illi mei tam
amanti, nec veſtræ nationis tot ingenioſis ſtudioſisꝗ adoleſcentibus, qui vehementer eum à me ef-
flagitare non deſinunt, vlla ratione poſſum. En igitur iam prodit cum in veſtram gratiam, tum in
omnium, qui hoc ſtudiorum genere delectantur, vtilitatem. Vos eum hilari fronte, vt grati animi
ſignum, accipite, &, quando me plane veſtrum eſſe perſpicitis, eandem, quam nunc vos habere
erga me voluntatem video, perpetuo conſeruate. Valete.

# HIERONYMI FABRICI

## A B

# AQVAPENDENTE

## ANATOMICI PATAVINI

## D E

# VENARVM

## OSTIOLIS.

**V**ENARVM* oſtiola à me nuncupantur, membranulæ aliquot tenuiſſimæ in interna cauitate venarum, quæ potiſſimùm in artus diſtribuuntur per interualla nunc ſingulatim, nunc geminatim diſpoſitæ, ac ſurſum quidem verſus venarum radicem, orificium habentes; infra autem cluſæ, & non diſſimilem formā exteriùs præſeſe rentes, * ac nodi in plantarum ramulis, & caule apparent . Ea rationé, vti opinor , à natura genitæ, vt ſanguinem quadantenus remorentur, ne confertim ac fluminis inſtar, aut ad pedes , aut in manus & digitos vniuerſus influat, colligaturq; ; duoq; incommoda eueniant, tum vt ſuperiores artuum partes alimenti penuria laborent; tum verò manus, & pedes tumore perpetuo premantur. Vt igitur iuſtiſſima menſura & admirabili quadam proportione ſanguis ad ſingulas partes alendas quoquouerſum diſtribuatur ; oſtiola venarum comparata fuere . De his itaque in præſentia locuturis , ſubit primum mirari, quomodo oſtiola hęc, ad hanc vsque ætatem tàm priſcos, quàm recentiores Anatomicos adeo latuerint ; vt non ſolùm nulla prorſus mentio de ipſis facta ſit , ſed neq; aliquis prius hæc viderit, quam Anno Domini ſeptuageſimo quarto, ſupra milleſimum & quingenteſimū, quo à me ſum ma cum lætitia inter diſſecandum obſeruata fuere ; quamuis diſſecandi profeſſio multos, atq; inſignes habuerit viros, qui accuratiſſimè ſingula quęq; rimati ſunt; qui tamen hac in re excuſandi quadantenus videntur . Quis enim vnquam fuiſſet opinatus intra venarum cauitatem reperiri poſſe membranas & oſtiola? cum pręſertim venarum cauitas , quę ad deferendum ſanguinem in corpus vniuerſum erat comparata, libera, vt liberè ſanguis permearet, futura eſſet: ſicuti quoq; arterijs vſu venit , quæ oſtiolis prorſus ſunt deſtitutæ, cum tamen quà canales ſunt , eandem ſubeant rationem, quam venæ: ſed & propter illud quoque excuſari decet Anatomicos , quia non ſunt oſtiola omnibus venis

A        tradita:

Tab.2
g. 4.

tradita: neq; enim \* Vena Caua, quà per corporis truncum perreptat, neque ✣ internæ iugulares, neq; itidem innumeræ externç, quæ \* exiguæ funt, oftiola habent. Contra verò quifpiam priores in re hac infimulauerit, quod vfum oftiolorum , qui apprimè videtur neceffarius indagare neglexerint, quoduè ipfa in venarum oftenfione non animaduerterint . nam nudis venis, ijsq; integris ante oculos oblatis oftiola fe fe quodammodo in confpectum exhibent : quinimmò quòd etiam in \* viuis brachijs ac cruribus oftiola de fe ipfis notitiâ præbeant, manifeftè apparet, quando miniftri ad fanguinem mittendû artus ligant. etenim per venarum interualla quidam veluti \* nodi exterius confpiciuntur, qui ab ipfis oftiolis conflantur: quibufdam verò vt baiulis , & rufticis, varicum modo in cruribus intumefcere videntur : immo , quod & ipfæ varices , non alia de caufa fiant , nifi quia fanguis craffior in oftiolis diutius detentus, oftiola, & venas dilatet, videtur neceffariò affeuerandum, quando fine oftiolis vniformiter quidem intumefcere, & dilatari venas par effet, non autem vti apparet varicum modo ; vt ex hoc alius quoq; oftiolorum vfus non contemnendus elucefcat, vt fcilicet robur indatur ipfis venis. Nam cum in varicibus, in quibus aut laxari, aut rumpi oftiola par eft , plus minusuè dilatatas femper venas confpiciamus, dicere proculdubio tutò poffumus ad prohibendam quoq; venarû diftenfionem fuiffe oftiola à fummo opifice fabrefacta : diftendi autem ac dilatari facilè potuiffent venæ, cum ex membranofa fubftantia eaque fimplici ac tenui fint conflatæ . Quod fi dilatarentur, præterquam quod multus fanguis inibi plus iufto cumulatus, & venas, & partes circumiacentes læderet, atq; in tumorem attolleret, vti euenire ijs compertum eft, quibus varices membris innafcuntur ; fuperioribus quoq; partibus quadantenus fubriperetur alimentum fanguine vtputa copiofo, quò dilatatû vas eft, præcipitante, & tanquam in lacuna referuato. Arterijs aût oftiola non fuere neceffaria , neq; ad diftenfionem prohibendâ propter tunicæ craffitiem , ac robur, neq; ad fanguinem remorandum quod fanguinis fluxus refluxusq; in arterijs perpetuo fiat. Sed age oftiolorum numerum, formam, conftitutionem, fitum, diftantiam, ac reliqua perpendamus . Erat profectò neceffaria oftiolorum conftructio in artuû venis, quæ non exiguæ, fed vel magnæ , vel moderatæ funt magnitudinis, vt fcilicet fanguis vbiq; eatenus retardetur, quatenus cuique particulæ alimento fruédi congruum tempus detur, quod alioqui propter artuû decliuem fitum confertim ac rapidi fluminis inftar in artuum extremitates vniuerfus conflueret, ac colligeretur, idq; tum harum partium tumore, tum fuperpofitarum marcore. Quod verò ab oftiolis fanguinis curfus retardetur; præterquamquod ipfa conftructio id patefacit, omnes quoq; poffunt periculum facere tum in nudis venis mortui corporis, tum in viuo artus ligantes, vt in miffione fanguinis fit. Si enim premere, aut deorfum fricádo adigere fanguinem tentes, curfum ipfius ab ipfis oftiolis intercipi , remorariq; apertè videbis : neq; enim aliter ego in huiufmodi notitiam fum deductus. Exiguæ autem venæ oftiolis non indigebant , tum propter earum paruitatem modicum fanguinis, ac totum, quod pro

ipfis

---

*Marginal notes (left):*

Oftiola vena rum in miffio ne fanguinie fe fe in confpectum quo exhibeant .

Varices quâ ob cauffam fiant .

Oftiolorum aliter vfus .

Arteriæ cur sarent oftiolis .

Oftiola retardant fangui nem .

Auctor quo in notitiam oftiolorû eft deductus .

*Marginal notes (right):*

\* Tab. KLM
† Tab B.
✲ Fig I. 3.

\* Tab fig. 1.
✲ Ta fig 1.

ipfis fatis eft,tantum modo continentes, tu quia fatis erat in maioribus
vafis ceu fonte immorari alimentum ; fic enim non defuturum etiã par-
uis quafi riuulis neceffarium erat. Porrò alia oftiolorum in artubus ne- *Oftiolorum in*
ceffitas eft. Nam cum crura, & brachia motu locali frequentiffimè e- *artubus ne-*
xerceantur, eoq; interdum vehementi, ac violentiffimo, vnde plurimũ, *ceffitas.*
ac vehementem in ipfis excitari calorem contingat; proculdubio vi ca-
loris excitati,fanguis ad artus in tanta copia fluxiffet,atq; attractus fuif-
fet; vt vel partibus principalibus ex Caua Vena fubriperetur alimentũ;
vel artuum vafa ruptionis periculo periclitarentur. Quorum vtrumque
maximè perniciofum toti animali erat futurum , quando principes par- *Partes prin-*
tes, vt hepar,cor, pulmones, & cerebrum,perpetuò fanguine abundare *cipes,cur fan*
copiofiffimo oportebat. Quam ob caufam vti opinor factum eft, vt ve- *guine abun-*
*dare debent.*
na * caua , quà per corporis truncum perreptat,fimiliter & * iugulares,
oftiolis prorfus fuerint deftitutæ. Decebat enim cerebrum,cor, pulmo
nes, hepar, ac renes,quæ totius animalis conferuationem procurant af-
fluere alimento, neq; ipfis retardari ne momentum quidem oportebat ,
tum ad deperditam fubftantiam refarciendam , tum ad gignendos vita-
les, atq; animales fpiritus, quorum caufa vita animalibus conferuatur.
Quod fi in + iugularium venarum origine oftiola in homine obferues ; *Oftiola vena*
ea ad fanguinem detinendum ,fne in decliui capitis fitu in cerebrum in- *rum iugula-*
*rium,ad quid*
ftar fluminis irruat, atque in eo plus iufto cumuletur,pofita effe dicas. *poffent effe*
His igitur de caufis oftiola artuum venis non quidem exiguis , fed me- *vtilia.*
diocribus, & magnis, fed neq; etiam venæ cauæ trunco, & iugularibus
tradita funt. Quod verò oftiola plerifq; locis fint pofita vbi fcilicet* ra *Oftiolorum*
mi minores fparguntur atq; obliquè propagantur;& hoc admirabilis eft *fitus.*
fapientiæ fpecimen : vt fcilicet eo loci fanguis moram trahat, quo opus
eft ipfum ad alias partes diftribuere, qui alioqui totus per vnicum am-
pliorem magifq; rectum ramum canalemque confluxiffet; quafi verò o-
ftiola folertes quoq; multarum partium ianitores exfiftant,ne fcilicet cõ
cedant inferius elabi ac defcendere alimentum, donec fuperiores partes
congruam illius portionem fint affecutæ. Forma oftiolorum ea eft, vt *Oftiolorum*
indicis, aut aliorum trium digitorum, vnguem imitentur, quæ meritò *forma.*
adaperta furfum verfus venaRum radicem fuere ; infra verò, atq; à lateri
bus venis ipfis coaluere. Cæterum fi quis in * Corde,aut magnæ arte
riæ,aut venæ arterialis oftiola viderit;horum omnium oftiolorum formã
fermè exactam habuerit, nifi quod in Corde tria, in venis verò,aut vni- *Oftiolorum*
ca, aut bina, fingulis locis funt conftituta:fimiliter in Corde craffiffima; *cordis & ve*
vt in diaftole, & fyftole, fufficerent;in venis vero tenuiffima confiftunt. *narum difcri*
*men.*
tenuiffima autem eft membrana oftiolorum,quia non decebat locũ fan- *Oftiolorum*
guinis magna ex parte occupari à membranis , quod vtiq; accidiffet, fi *cur membra-*
craffiori membrana fuiffent conflata . Verum & illud infuper eft adno *na tenuiffima*
tandum,quod fumma cum tenuitate,fumma etiam denfitas adiuncta fit,
quod factum eft ad oftiolorum fecuritatem,ac patiendi difficultatem, ne *Oftiola cur*
videlicet incurfu fanguinis valido, ac præcipiti, vbi fcilicet in huiufmo- *denfiffima.*
di valuulas impingeret, rumperentur.De quarum fanè denfitate,ac robo
re,ipfæ varices indicio funt. Si enim fanguinem denfum,craffum,& pó

A 2    derofum,

derosum, qualis melancholicus est, multo tépore detinent sustinéntq; :
proculdubio robustas esse huiusmodi membranas fatendum est. quod si
quis etiam violentia quadam tentet, sanguinem deorsum per venas im-
pellere, resistentiam, & ostiolorum robur experiretur. * Bina autem

' Tab,
rè oé

*Ostiolorum
numerus.* ostiola singulis locis passim sunt apposita, non sicut in Corde tria,quia
in corde recursum magis impediri, in venis transitum aliqua ex parte re
morari erat opus : in corde rursus magna aderat diastole, & systole , in
venis nulla : in corde tandem maxima sunt foramina canalesq; amplissi
mi, vbi ostiola adsunt: ob quam causam in boue, vt puta vasto animali,
*Cur ostiola
in venis ad
summū bina.* aliquando tria obseruata sunt ostiola. Quod si duo in venis ostiola sa-
tis erant, superuacuum erat tria constituere.Satis autem erant duo, quia
duo paululum retardare validum sanguinis cursum, nequaquam autem
impedire transitum poterant: propter hoc loca etiam passim non pauca
*Cur in quibuf
dā venis fin-
gulas.* adsunt, quibus * vnicum tantum ostiolum conformatum est,vt scilicet
iustissima fiat sanguinis retardatio . Nam vbi plus remorari ipsum con
uenicns erat, duo; vbi minus, vnum tantum ostiolum fuit substitutum.

*Tab,
rè oé

*Tab,
rè o

Potissimum autem + vnum apponitur; vbi natura ex maiori ramo aliquod minus vas obliquè est propagatura. tunc enim in maiori ramo,pau
lo sub orificio minoris propagati ramuli, ostiolum quasi septum confor-
matur, vt scilicet sanguis descendens ab ostiolo non solum detineatur ,
verum etiam in ipsum impulsus retrò gurgitet, & quasi stagnans in ve-
*Similitudo o-
stiolorum ab
obstaculis
quf aquam in
molendinis
detinēt .* nulæ ostium ingrediatur. Similem sanè industriam hic natura machina-
ta, atque in molendinarum machinis ars molitur, in quibus artifices vt
aqua multa detineatur, ac pro molendinarum, ac machinarum vsu refer
uetur, obstacula nonnulla, quæ latinè septa,& claustra,vulgo autē clau-
sas,& rostas vocant, apponunt, in quibus maxima aquæ copia , atq; in
summa ea, quæ necessaria est,veluti in apto ventre colligitur: æquè profectò natura in venis ipsis, quæ veluti fluuiorum canales sunt per ostiola, tum singula, tum geminata molitur. Neq; hoc loco quispiam admi
retur, quod natura passim * ostiola potissimum geminata paret, vbi in
*Situs ostio-
lorum.* venæ trunco nullus obliquè ramus propagatur ,cum tamen ostiolorum
necessitas sit, sanguinem pro illis ipsam quodammodo detinendo reser-
uare; quoniam non tantum ad sanguinem pro obliquis ramorum orifi-
cijs stagnandum, ac reseruandum, quantum ad eundem in itinere remo
randum, ne impetu deorsum vniuersus labatur, excurratq;, ostiola in
venis posita sunt . ideo oportuit serie multa ostiola esse, & singula paululum conferentia, non modo ad præcipitantem sanguinem remorandum vti dictum est, sed etiam ad venarum distentionem vbiq; prohiben
dam . Verum enimuero, hic quoq; æquum est naturæ industriam admi
rari: * duo enim ostiola mutuò sibi proxima facta sunt,atq; tam magna,
vt plusquam dimidiam venarum cauitatem contineant, oppleantq;: reliqua verò dimidia libera est,& ostiolis prorsus destituta: propter hoc,
aliquid non obstabat, quominus sanguis confertim fluere per liberam
vasis partem deorsum valeret, atq; incommoda,quæ relata sunt, impor-
*Distantia o-
stiolorum .* taret.Ob id natura, præterquam quod ostiola plurima per vasis longitudinem, duorum, trium, quattuorue digitorum interuallo distantia com-
parauit,

*'T
O.
bi.

*
fig

*
fig

parauit; inuenit infuper, mirabilem quandam artem, quo fanguinis va-
lidus curfus retardaretur. Nam plùra quidem, atq; ex eodem latere, fiue per rectam lineam difpofita oftiola, moram vel nullam, vel admodū
leuem effeciffent; quia fanguis totus rectà per vafis liberam partem con
fluxiffet. Quod fi fingulis locis tribus, quattuorue oftiolis, omnem intus
cauitatem oppleuiffet; tunc fanguinis tranfitum omninò impediuiffet.
Proinde natura, ita oftiola difpofuit, vt perpetuo fuperiora inferioribus, *Difpofitio o-*
& fibi proximis aduerfam fubinde pofitionem obtinuerint, non diffimi *ftiolorū quo-*
li ratione, atq; in * herbis ipfis, flores, folia, & ramufculos fubinde à cau *lis.*
lis contraria regione enafci videntur. Sic enim inferiora * oftiola fem
per quod à fuperioribus elabitur, remorantur, interim vero fanguinis
tranfitus non impeditur. Vltimo loco de oftiolis illud eft indagandum,
qui fiat, vt in alijs frequentiora numeroq; plura, tùm in cruribus, tum
in brachijs confpiciantur oftiola, in alijs pauciora: id quod manifeftif- *Oftiola cur*
mè patet, cum miniftri in viuo homine fanguinis euacuandi gratia artus *in fanguinis*
*miffione in*
ligant. Dicendum eft, plura confpici in ijs, qui aut melancholico fan- *alijs plura,*
guine craffiffimo, aut contrà, biliofo ac tenuiffimo abundant (in quibus *in alijs pau-*
cafibus, vfus oftiolorum, fiue fanguinis tenuis fluxilisq; remorandi gra- *ciora appa-*
tia, fiue craffi prohibendi, ne venam diftenderet, magis viget) aut rur- *reant.*
fus in ijs qui corporis magnitudine pollent: aut carnofi magis funt, eoq;
venas habent numerofiores, vt vfu oftiolorum ad fanguinem obliquis
ramis porrigendum magis indigeant: aut vafa habent latiffima, quæ o-
ftiola multa poftulant, vt fanguinis curfus magis remoretur, roburq; ve
nis accedat: aut longas rectasq; venas partes fortiuntur, ne longitudi-
nis, rectitudinisq; caufa, fanguis multus, impetu quodam inftar fluminis rectà feratur, fed remoretur: aut tandem fi animal mobilitate promp-
tius natura fit, plura funt oftiola comparata. Atque hæc eft meo marte *Tabulæ oftio*
in re noua inuenta naturæ fapientia, & artificium. Quot autem nume- *lorum necef-*
ro fint oftiola in quaq; vena, & quomodo in ipfis partibus fint difpofi- *farig.*
ta, ac pleraq; alia, ex ipfa magis Tabularum infpectione, quàm hiftoriâ
innotefcent.

# TABVLAE

# TABVLAE PRIMAE

## DE OSTIOLIS VENARVM

# Explanatio.

*TABVLA PRIMA in dimidio ferè brachio nonnulla oſtiola
venarum oſtendit. Omnia enim, maluimus tantum in crure
exſequi, ne tractatus hic exiguus excreſceret in nimiam multitudinem figurarum. Imprimis ergo ad interna iugularis exortum
ſcilicet in inferno colli termino, ſunt bina oſtiola A. , & ante ipſa,
vena maximum orificium, E. E. in ſola vero iugulari A.B.D.
ſupra hæc duo memorata oſtiola A. nulla alia viſuntur, niſi glandula ſub aure D. neq; in ramo B. C. aliquod exſtat oſtiolum, niſi orificium mediocre. Poſt bina autem iſta oſtiola A. in vena
axillari F. G. vnum grande ſequitur oſtiolum H. Vnde, facta vena axillaris F. G. diuiſione, in Cephalicam ſeu humerariam G. I.
& in Baſilicā ſiue iecorariam G. K : in Cephalica quidem G. I.
per exteriorem brachÿ partem, ſub L. R. M. I. Deltoide muſculo, perreptante : duo adſunt oſtiola L. & M. quinq; ferè digitis
mutuò inter ſe diſtantia, quorum primum L, ad principium, alterum M. ad finem Deltoidis L. R. M. I. ponitur. In Baſilica verò ſiue Hepatica G. K. per interiorem brachÿ partem progrediente; quatuor oſtiola N. O. P. Q. ſatis magna conformantur, quorum ſecundum O. à primo N. quatuor digitorum interuallo diſtat; tertium P. à ſecundo O. trium; quartum Q. à tertio P. duorum, tum ſuccedunt duo parua oſtiola K.*

*Obiter autem in hac figura notantur.*

*S.S.S.S.S. quinque coſta abſciſa.*

*T. axilla ſeu ala brachÿ.*

*V. Muſculus qui vulgò Piſcis vocatur.*

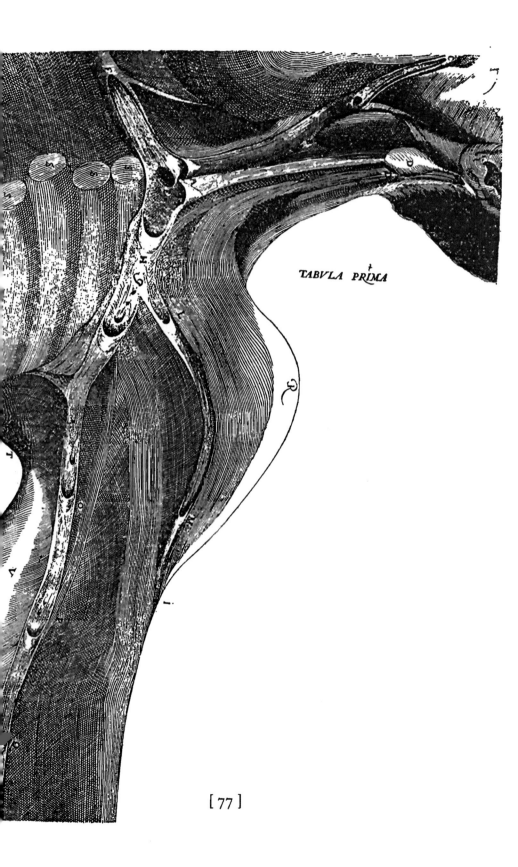

TABVLA PRIMA

# TABVLAE SECVNDAE

## DE VENARVM OSTIOLIS

# Explanatio.

*SECVNDA TABVLA, quæ eſt ceterarum maxima, & apprimè neceſſaria, quinq́, continet figuras.*

*FIGVRA I. exhibet Brachium viuum, ſuperiùs vinculo adſtriƈtum, vt in miſſione ſanguinis fieri ſolet, apparetq; in eo portio Cephalica ſeu humeraria A. B. & portio Baſilica ſeu iecoraria C.D, tum vena Communis vulgò Mediana vocata E.F. in qua,quemadmodum in alijs,videntur oſtiola O O.O.veluti no di quidam. Sic enim in viuis brachijs, oſtiola venarum ſeſe exteriùs conſpicienda exhibent.*

*FIGVRA II. porrigit duas venas crurum inuerſas, A.B.& C.D. vt ex ijs manifeſtentur oſtiola,O.O.O.quomodo intus in cauitate venarum conſiſtant. Priuatim verò, ex inſpeƈtione harum inuerſarum venarum, hoc ſingulare apparet ; quod priora ſuperioraq; oſtiola,ſubſequentibus ſibi proximis,perinde aduerſam poſitionem obtinent ,ac in plantis rami, ut ex Tertia figura appa rebit . Prætera,in hac Figura ſecundo,hoc animaduertendum eſt, in prima ſeu ſuperiori cruris vena A.B.eſſe oſtiola O O O. xylo ſeu goſſipio repleta; vt melius conſpicerentur: in ſecunda verò cruris vena C.D.oſtiola O.O.O.vacua ſunt.*

*FIGVRA III. in qua nodi N.N.N. abſciſorum ramorum plantæ conſpiciuntur, appoſita eſt,ut in ſecunda figura admonuimus : ut comparatio oſtiolorum, cum exortu ramorum,clarior euadat.*

*FIGVRA IIII. Plantam exhibet eam,quæ Verbena di citur. Eſt enim herba hæc, vulgò cognitiſſima,à qua in figura ter tia , rami abſciſi fuerunt .*

*FIGVRA V. eſt iecoris A. A. diſſeƈti, vt trunci vena caua B.B.B.B.& venæ portæ C.C.C.propè veſicam fellis D. in conſpe ƈtum*

ctum venirent, & priores grandioresq; vtrius q; vena rami, vide-
rentur; eo potissimùm nomine, ut studiosi animaduerterent, ea disse-
ctioni non conuexire, qua à quodā, qui ante me scripsit, posteris tradita sunt. Videlicet, in vena caua B.B.B.B. & vena porta C.C.C
truncis ac exortibus, à iecore A.A. emergentibus; inueniri Apo
physes membranarum, si niles valuulis, qua in Corde adsunt . Etenim ijs verbis, potuisset quispiam, ad truncos & exortus pradicta
rum venarum, existimare adesse ostiola, cū ad sensum nulla prorsus appareant , sed statim à trunco vtriusq; uena , Porta scilicet
C. C. C. & Caua B. B. B. B. grandes rami, quorum foramina
uidentur, statim expullulent , intusq; in iecoris A. A. substantiam
digerantur .

TABVLÆ. ii FIGVRA i BRACHII VIVI AD SANGVI:

A. B · *Porfio Cephalica* · C· D · *Porfio basilica* · E F · *Vena Com:*

B

D

*A. B* *prima cura.*

FIGVRA. ii DVARV

*C D altera* o o o *articolo* te:

N                          N          FIGVRA

N. *articli absciforum venarum q*

FIGVRA iiii.
V *Vertena*

V

R          R

V

V. *Plata*
R R R R   Ro:

ii

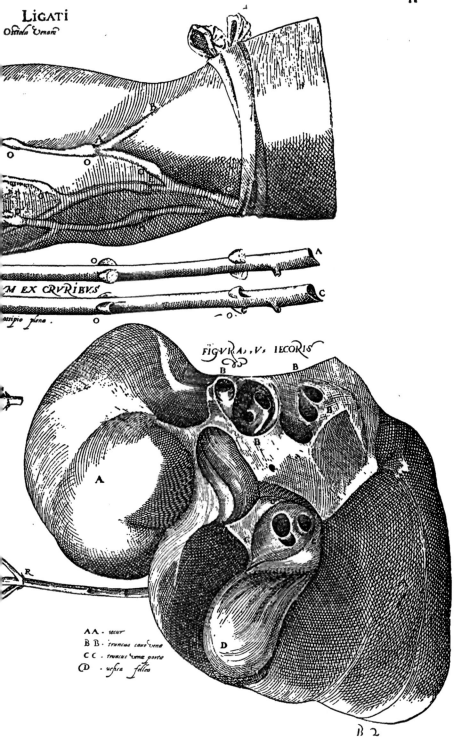

LIGATI
*Ostiola Venam*

*M EX CRVRIBVS*
*ossipio plena.*

FIGVRA, V. IECORIS

AA. *secut*
BB. *truncus cauæ venæ*
CC. *truncus venæ portæ*
CD. *uesica fellea*

B 2

# TABVLAE TERTIAE
## DE OSTIOLIS VENARVM
# Explanatio.

TABVLA TERTIA, in superna sui parte, exhibet Cor
A. B. C. diuisum ad sinistrum ventriculum A.D.E.C.
vt appareant sua fibra D. E. atq; videantur ad exortum aorta
seu magna arteria tria ostiola F.F.F. deinde, vt in tota magna
arteria G. H. I. per corporis truncum diuisa, plurima conspician
tur à superna vsq; ad infernam sui partem foramina, qua nihil
aliud sunt quam rami eiusdem ad spina partes & alto propagati. Hac ergo magna arteria quemadmodum & cateri sui rami,
nulla continet ostiola. Sed & vena caua K. L. M. N. magna
arteria F. G. H. I. propinqua quà parte per corporis truncum
perreptat & vnica est atq; maxima, nullum pariter sortita est
ostiolum, ob quam caussam, tota hic diuisa est. In eius autem superna parte, duo adsunt magna foramina R. & S. in hepar in-
gredientia, qua postmodum, inferius sequitur vnum emulgentis
vena dextra foramen M. & paullò post sinistra emulgens O.
patet aperta, ad renem P: sinistrum pertinens, & ostiolis destituta.

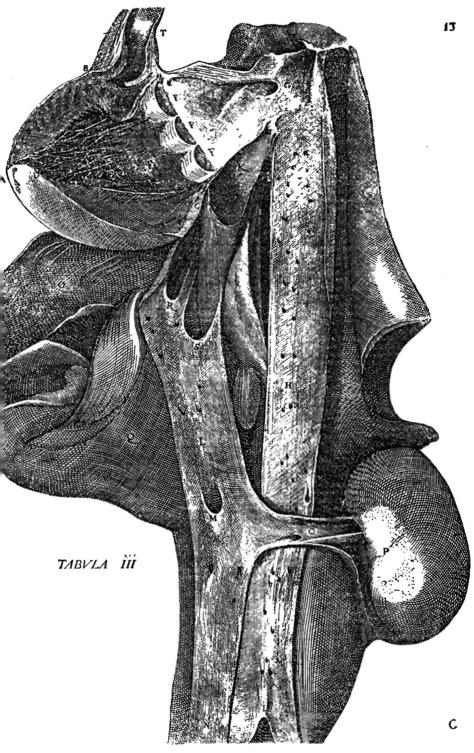

TABVLA ÏÏÏ

C

# TABVLAE QVARTAE

## DE VENARVM OSTIOLIS

# Explanatio.

Q*VARTA TABVLA, & in cruris ordine prima,
duas figuras continet, quæ in interna parte totius cruris
à coxa vsq; ad pedem ferè, nobis exhibent ostiola duorum ramorum, quorum alter interior & aliquanto maior est,
A B. B G. alter exterior & paullò minor D E. E H. Interior
A B. B G. Popliti I. propinquior conspicitur, habens quinq, ostio
la L.M.N.O.P. per interualla certa ita disposita; ut tantum singula sint à superna parte A. ad eam partem infernam P. ubi
multum poplitis I. multumq; ipsius genu K. præterijsset. Postea à
Q ad B. succedunt bina in prima figura; & in altera figura in
fine cruris, prope pedem, adest unicum tantum R. Atq; omnia
unica ostiola, ramum obliquè propagatum obtinent L.M.N.O.P.
& in altera figura R.G. bina uerò Q. & B. nequaquam.*

*Alter ramus D. E. exterior, ab anteriore coxa productus,
genu K. propior, aliquantulum progressus à D. ad S. bina primũ
parua ostiola continet, inde usq; sub genu quatuor T.V.X.Z.
eaq; omnia singula quidem, sed tamen ita disposita, ut tria T.V.X
duorum digitorum interuallo inter se distent, quartum autem Z.
à tertio X. quatuor digitorum spatium habeat. Atq; ubi sunt pri
mò bina osticla S. & ultimum Z. ibi ramus obliquè propagatur,
in alijs intermedijs ostiolis T.V.X. nequaquam:*

[ 84 ]

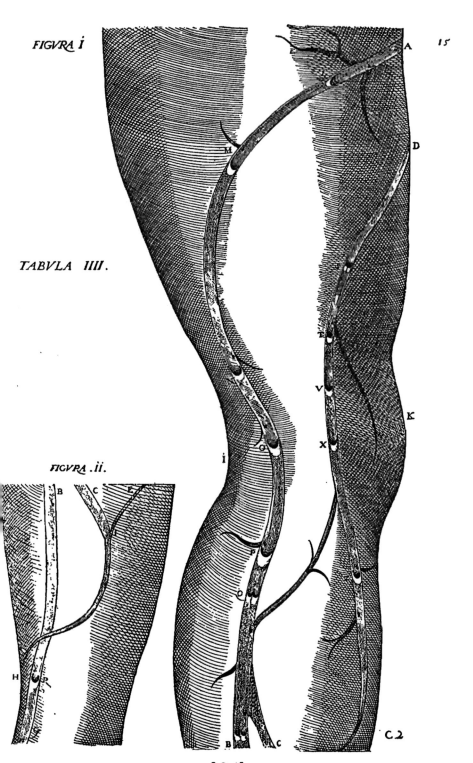

FIGVRA i

TABVLA IIII.

FIGVRA .ii.

# TABVLAE QVINCTAE
## DE OSTIOLIS VENARVM
# Explanatio.

TABVLA QVINCTA, cum duabus sequentibus vi
delicet, cum sexta & septima talem habet connexionem, vt
si ad inferiorem quincta Tabula extremitatem B. C. supremam
sexta tabula extremitatem B. C. applicuisses, & postmodum in-
ferna extremitati sexta tabula D. iunxisses extremitatem superio
rem D. Tabula septima ; composuisses integrum crus humanum
A.B.C.D.E. Atq̃ in his tribus tabulis simul iunctis , videres
vno intuitu multa vniuersi cruris ostiola partim interna partim
externa, qua nunc separatim in vnaquaq; tabula videbis .

FIGVRA itaq; Tabula quincta, commonstrat venam
& arteriam coxendicis, à bifurcatis truncis I. K. L. M. &
A.H.F.G. per vtriusq; longitudinem diuisam, vt conspicere pos-
sis venam I.K.L.M.N.B. N.C. ostiola habere, Arteriam verò
A.H.F.G. prorsus ijs destitui . Vena ergò L.M. quousq; v-
nica persistit vsq; ferè ad inguina M.O. bina sortitur ostiola, dein
de diuisa bifariam N. B. N.C. Pars quidem profundior & maior N. C. duobus locis bina habet ostiola, quatuor ferè digitis in-
terse distantia, deinde ad C. occultatur . Pars verò minor in bi-
furcationis initio N. primùm continet bina ostiola ; deinde duorũ
digitorum interuallo alia bina ; rursus trium digitorum interstitio
alia bina ; donec quarto loco , quatuor digitorum spatio vnicum
ostiolum consistat . quod Figura Tabula sexta demonstrabit .

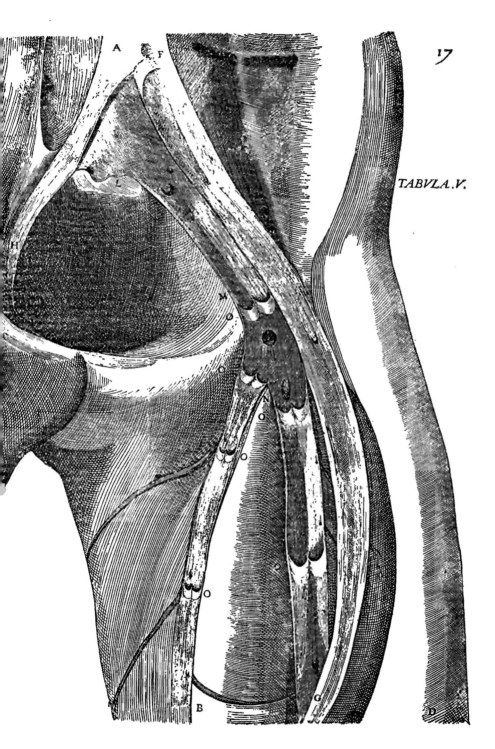

17

TABVLA.V.

# TABVLAE SEXTAE

## DE VENARVM OSTIOLIS

# Explanatio.

TABVLA SEXTA cum pracedenti in B.C.continua tionem habens,vnicam tantum venam B.P.Q.R.S.T.D ostendit, qua est pars minoris rami, proueniens ex bifurcatione ve na in sexta tabula explicata, & constituens Saphenam,in qua sta tim adest ostiolum vnicum P. quod quarto loco quatuor digitorū spatio conformatum est , inter ostiola,præcedenti Tabula explica ta . Ab hoc deinde ostiolo P. bina sese exhibent Q. habentia supra se ramulum α, ε, obliquè propagatum. Postea quatuor digitorum interstitio ferè sub poplite, bina rursus ostiola R. sine vllo ramo visuntur . Sub his, trium digitorum interuallo vnicum qui dem producitur ostiolum S. verùm ante se obliquum habet ramulum γ. δ. ε. Et ab hoc rursus ostiolo S. quatuor digitorum interuallo,adest aliud T.ante se itidem habens ramulum ζ. η. Deniq, quin que digitorum ferè spatio in sequenti figura, qua cum hac Tabula in D. continuatur,videbis adesse ostiolum,si conuertes folium.

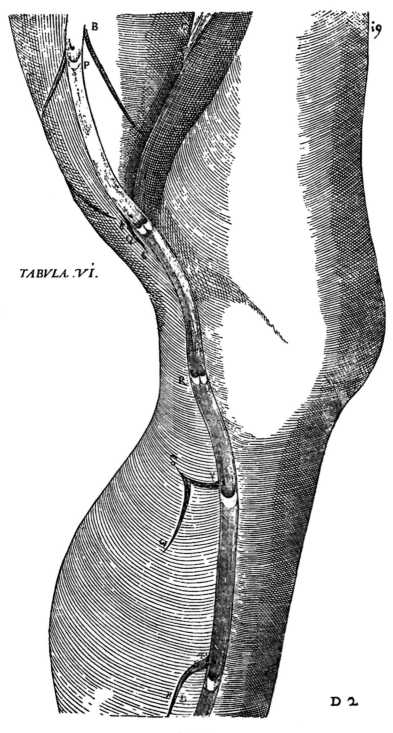

TABVLA .VI.

D 2

# TABVLAE SEPTIMAE

## DE VENARVM OSTIOLIS

# Explanatio.

TABVLA SEPTIMA *continuata cum præcedenti in D. in eadem Saphena D. E. ab oftiolo præcedentis Tabulæ vltimo, quinq; digitorum ferè fpatio habet oftiolum V. cum fuo ramo θ·ι· obliquè ante fe propagato. Deinde totius pedis X. Y. Z. D. oftiola fupernè interneq́ per pedem progredientia demon ſtrat, & primò ad talum κ. λ. oftendit bina oftiola X. quæ fupra fe hinc inde habent orificia duorum propagatorum ramorum κ μ. λ. τ. Ab hoc gemino oftiolo X. trium ferè digitorum interuallo vnicum adeſt oftiolum Y. cum adnata ante fe propagine venæ ξ & eadem ferè diſtantia vltimum eiufdem faphenæ oftiolum Z. confpicitur, itidem cum adnata fibi propaginæ venæ π· verùm fitu differenti quàm fuit propago ξ tandem vena Z. E. fine vllis oftiolis vfq; ad fummum magni digiti cacumen E. procurrit, finem Saphenæ conſtituens.*

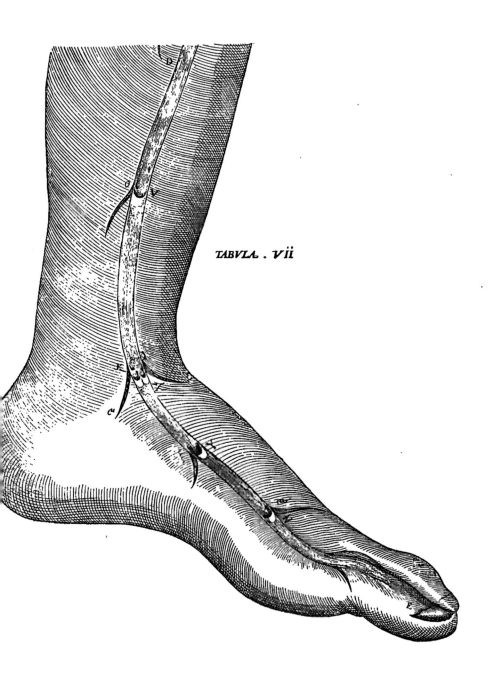

TABVLA . VII

# TABVLAE OCTAVAE

## DE VENARVM OSTIOLIS

# Explanatio.

*T*ABVLA OCTAVA *demonſtrat oſtiola partis maio-*
*ris eius rami qui proueniebat ex bifurcatione vena cum ar-*
*teria progredientis & iam explicata in Sexta Tabula, qua fuit ſe-*
*cunda Tabularum cruris . Etenim eius vena ramus internus*
*maior A. B. qui interiùs verſus internam coxa partem excurrēs*
*cum arteria B.C. ramo magno, hac ratione progreditur, vt in hac*
*Tabella depingitur, omniaꝗ hac profert oſtiola D.E.F.G.H.I.*
*primum quidem bina B, cum ramulo* α, *deinde alia bina E. cum*
*ramulo* β. *tertio loco ad poplitem K. vnicum magnum F. cum*
*ramulo ante ſe propagato* γ *quarto loco, ad cruris partem carno-*
*ſam L. qua ſura dicitur, oſtiola bina G. ſine vllo ramulo; quinĉto lo-*
*co vnicum H. cum adnatis ramulis* δ. ε. *Sexto loco bina oſtiola I.*
*eaꝗ ſine ramulis, ſub his, vena bifariā B. M. & B. N. diuiditur.*
*Atꝗ ha propoſita tabula, quia ſatis eſſe poſſunt ad cōmoſtran-*
*dam admirabilem natura induſtriam qua vſa fuit in propagan-*
*dis oſtiolis; ideo a plurium oſtiolorum qua ſuperſunt delineatione*
*ſuperſedendum putauimus, hic finem facientes .*

# Superiorum Permiſſu.

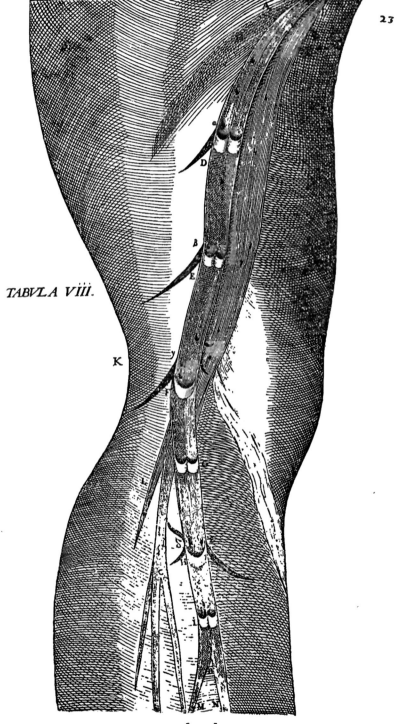

TABVLA VIII.

# SIZES OF ORIGINAL PLATES

All measurements are in inches.

The first page, which is a facsimile of the title-page of 1603, is a right-hand page. The dedication page, which backs the title page, is a left-hand page. Then follow pages one to twenty-three, with odd-number pages being on the right, and even-number pages on the left. The large plate occupied two pages.

The original copper plates used were not always rectangles, nor are their edges always clearly marked in printing. Each plate therefore has been listed on its merits.

SIZES

Title page, 1625
Width     8.45 inches
Length 12.60 inches

Title page, 1603
Width     5.34 inches
Length 10.00 inches

Dedication page, 1603
Width     5.33 inches
Length   8.96 inches

Page 1
Width     5.65 inches
Length 10.70 inches

Page 2
Width     5.70 inches
Length 10.70 inches

Page 3
Width     5.65 inches
Length 10.60 inches

Page 4
Width     5.70 inches
Length 10.65 inches

Page 5
Width     5.70 inches
Length 10.25 inches

Page 6
Width     5.60 inches
Length   8.20 inches

Page 7
Width, top         10.70 in.
Width, bottom 10.30 in.
Length, left       15.75 in.
Length, right      15.70 in.

Page 8
Width     5.70 inches
Length 10.85 inches

Page 9
Width     5.65 inches
Length   3.00 inches

Pages 10 and 11
  Width, top        20.75 in.
  Width, bottom 21.10 in.
  Length, left      14.85 in.
  Length, right    15.10 in.

Page 12
  Width    5.7 inches
  Length  6.15 inches

Page 13
  Width    9.10 inches
  Length 15.40 inches

Page 14
  Width    5.70 inches
  Length  7.53 inches

Page 15
  Width, top        6.50 in.
  Width, bottom  7.80 in.
  Length            15.83 in.

Page 16
  Width    5.74 inches
  Length  7.50 inches

Page 17
  Width, top        7.80 in.
  Width, bottom  6.93 in.
  Length, center 13.68 in.

Page 18
  Width    5.75 inches
  Length  6.00 inches

Page 19
  Width    7.30 inches
  Length 13.85 inches

Page 20
  Width    5.73 inches
  Length  5.70 inches

Page 21
  Width, top        3.95 in.
  Length, right    11.90 in.

Page 22
  Width    5.70 inches
  Length  8.00 inches

Page 23
  Width, top        7.20 in.
  Width, bottom  5.15 in.
  Length            15.60 in.

# INDEX

CPSIA information can be obtained
at www.ICGtesting.com
Printed in the USA
LVOW10s1453240717
542438LV00037B/1740/P